# Stranger at the Door
Writers and the Act of Writing

# Stranger at the Door
Writers and the Act of Writing

Kristjana Gunnars

Wilfrid Laurier University Press

We acknowledge the support of the Canada Council for the Arts for our publishing program. We acknowledge the financial support of the Government of Canada through the Book Publishing Industry Development Program for our publishing activities. We acknowledge the Government of Ontario through the Ontario Media Development Corporation's Ontario Book Initiative.

ONTARIO ARTS COUNCIL
CONSEIL DES ARTS DE L'ONTARIO

Library and Archives Canada Cataloguing in Publication

Gunnars, Kristjana, 1948–
    Stranger at the door : writers and the act of writing / Kristjana Gunnars.

Includes bibliographical references.
ISBN 0-88920-455-1

1. Creative writing.  2. Authorship.  3. Authors.  I. Title.

PN149.G85 2004                    808'.02                    C2004-906176-3

Cover design by P.J. Woodland. Text design by C. Bonas-Taylor.

Printed in Canada

Order from:
Wilfrid Laurier University Press
Wilfrid Laurier University
Waterloo, Ontario, Canada  N2L 3C5
www.wlupress.wlu.ca

# Contents

# Preface and Acknowledgements

This collection of essays evolved during a decade spent as a professor of creative writing at the University of Alberta. Everyone knows that teaching creative writing is a mixed bag that involves everything, and you can never be sure how it will go or whether it will be useful or not. One of the great obstacles for teaching in the creative fields, as Theodor Adorno mentions in his essay "Taboos on the Teaching Vocation," is the natural "antipathy toward the regimentation that is imposed" by the educational system itself (*Critical Models* 177). Creative work needs to be free and unhampered by outside voices. The writer needs to feel the confidence of his or her own voice, which is often taken away in the classroom—invariably far too early. Students are, in fact—in Adorno's own phrase—not even considered "legal subjects having fully equal rights" (181) with their teachers and administrators. In an environment where "spirit is reduced to a commodity" (182) and where the lineage of the teacher is drawn from both the monk, the jailer, and the drill sergeant, and where he or she is simultaneously regarded as "a kind of cripple" (183), teaching writing may be simply absurd. There is the possibility that the school, with its enclosed systems of thought and regulations, may be mistaken for reality, and this is deadly for creativity, which gets its lifeblood from sensitivity to the world around us. Indeed, Adorno says succinctly what many students voice in their own ways: that "what occurs in school remains far below the pupils' passionate expectations" (187). Here is Adorno's shattering assessment, in fact, of the teaching vocation and its ties to the learning vocation: "One hears again and again—and this I wish only to register, without presuming to pass judgment—that student teachers during their training period are broken, cast in the same mold, that their *élan*, all that is best in them, is destroyed (189)."

For Adorno, this is a political matter. The problem with education as a destruction of the soul is of critical importance because the schools and universities have an obligation to refrain from producing and encouraging people who would participate in, for example, genocide. In his essay "Education After Auschwitz," he speaks of "the administered world" and how it produces a "fury against civilization"(193). "The only education," he claims, "that has any sense at all is an education toward critical self-reflection" (193). It is on this point that the learning and teaching of creative writing, for all the obstacles and frequent absurdities such education is faced with—based as it is on the talking seminar and the intense analysis of words and sentences and logic and thoughts and ideas in a text—is incredibly valuable. My contention is that the writing seminar just might be the most valuable place in the entire school, for what goes on there is at the heart of what education should do: it takes the student, and inevitably also the teacher, on a journey "toward critical self-reflection." Adorno goes so far as to insist that "the single genuine power standing against the principle of Auschwitz" is the ability to acquire "the power of reflection, of self-determination" (195). He points out that the "educational ideal of hardness, in which many may believe without reflecting about it, is utterly wrong" (197). The creative arts—writing, editing, composing—are the very thing we do to combat that hardness embattling us on all sides. Writers are, and should be, profoundly sensitive to others, and to the emotions of others. Says Adorno, quite rightly for the fostering of writing, "an education must be promoted that no longer sets a premium on pain and the ability to endure pain" (198). He envisions an education that does not foster our repressions but allows them to be aired and respected—lest they be displaced into rage or manipulativeness or sadism. We fetishize technology and order and efficiency, and these are anathema to the creative soul. What we attempt to do in the writing room is, to put it bluntly, "an exhortation to love" (202). It is no surprise that creative writing as a discipline suffers humiliations in the academy, but it is also a remarkable feat that this field of endeavour not only goes on in the university, but even thrives and grows as well.

There is a good essay on these issues, specific to creative writing in the academy, by Madison Smartt Bell, which is his introduction to a textbook called *Narrative Design: A Writer's Guide to Structure*. Bell talks about the "paradox" of learning creative writing; learning writing is different from all other fields of study because "you will not encounter universal axioms and theorems, as in mathematics, or a fixed corpus of information to be learned, as in history, or even a generally agreed-upon set of rules for procedure, as in expository writing. More likely you will find yourself adrift in a cloud of conflicting opinions" (3). You have to get used to being "adrift" and uncertain. Bell argues that "the lack of fixity, the flux of most creative writing classes, permits at least some kind of freedom—but freedom can be a spooky thing to handle" (3). While the idea of a writing workshop is good, he notes, "there are snakes in the garden" (5). There is no consensus, for one thing; and there is little recognition of real success when it occurs, because everything is geared towards the critique. The students—and the teacher—have to tread the line carefully between the creative process—which is highly private and solitary—and the act of critical analysis—which is a group activity.

Since I myself walked that tightrope for several years, I've had ample opportunity to ponder the various formulations of the marriage between creative writing and academic literary studies. It was because the "paradoxes" were on my mind all the time that I ended up making notes to myself on writing and life and learning—on reading the works of respected and accomplished writers in the public sphere. Those notes eventually led to the essays collected here. More than this, however, these essays are really an outgrowth of conversations with students. The task at hand, under whatever circumstance, has always been to keep the conversation going and the writing happening. It was especially the graduate courses that provided me with the milieu in which the creative and the intellectual could mix—and the real relationship between the creative and the analytical found its form. But in this field, learning goes on at the strangest moments, and creative writing is an education that involves the whole person. Because of that fact, many interesting (and some strange) things occur along the way. We all get inspired, find it difficult, and hit the wall at various times. But the creative writing seminar and the spin-offs of those classes—casual conversations over coffee, discussions and manuscript readings in the office, the question and answer periods after official readings by visiting writers, correspondence—can contain the most valuable part of this kind of education.

During a sabbatical in 1996 I almost accidentally started the first of these essays, and have continued to add to them over the next five years. That first year I was asked by Dr. Sissel Lie, professor of French language and literature at NTNU in Trondheim, Norway, to attend a creative writing seminar being held in the village of Steinkjer. She asked me to talk abut the uses of theory in fictional texts. Out of this commission came the first of these essays, "Theory and Fiction: The Mixed Bag of Postmodern Writing." I read the essay to the group and we discussed our ideas. Later I incorporated notes from those discussions into the text. Over time, those notes have been added to from further readings and more conversations with colleagues and students. In May of 2001, I offered this paper in a much rewritten form to a seminar at the University of Göteborg in Sweden, at the instigation of Dr. Hans Löfgren, who was organizing academic seminars for faculty and graduate students in the English department there. The paper was handed out beforehand and we discussed it during the meeting. Many interesting points were raised on the issues of ethics, multiculturalism, and women's writing. The same process occurred with the second essay in this collection. Dr. Petra Von Morstein, professor of philosophy at the University of Calgary, was directing the Apeiron Society for the Practice of Philosophy, a public association of philosophically minded readers. She asked me to speak to the society in Calgary, and I went there twice in two years. In the first instance, I read an early version of a paper on authorship. The second time, I read a version of the essay included here, "The Diasporic Imagination." Both occasions were rewarding for me as an essay writer, because the feedback was good and the audience was very involved. I was able to take back with me some concerns, in particular about multiculturalism, and rewrite the article.

Towards the end of that sabbatical, I started two of the other essays included here. One was something I had wanted to write on for a long time, which became "The Art of Simplicity," and which eventually turned into "The Art of Solitude." There seemed to be a strong connection between the solitary writer and the monk, the poet, and the hermit. I went ahead and pursued the thought, which took its own direction. Since I began that line of inquiry, I have found innumerable instances where a similar case is made by other writers—such as Marguerite Duras, who in her book *Writing* likens the writer's need for solitude to "being alone in a shelter during the war" (15). I benefitted strongly from informal conversations on this subject, among others, over lunches and dinners with poet Tim Lilburn, who was writer-in-residence at the University of Alberta during 1998-99. Another of these essays, which I called "Writing and Silence: The Unteachable Mystery of Words," was begun after reading the new release of Maurice Blanchot's essays in English. I began to write this essay in response to some of Blanchot's ideas, and this became an ongoing interest. The following year I read this paper to the Department of English at the

University of Alberta. This essay, in an earlier version, was translated into Norwegian by Dr. Sissel Lie and published in Norwegian in *Skrivingens Rom* at NTNU.

The essay "Home and the Artist" was written purely for my own enjoyment. I had been interested in the idea of home and its relation to writing ever since first reading Virginia Woolf's essay "A Room of One's Own." The idea that one must go to a writing retreat, of which there are many, in order to be able to write always struck me as impossible from a lifestyle point of view. Writing and life seem so merged, so inseparable, that parcelling out chunks of time from "real life" in order to write did not seem nearly as good an idea to me as it does to many others. I tended to agree with Stephen King, who says in his book *On Writing*, "you need the room, you need the door, and you need the determination to shut the door" (157). So I attempted to find out how artists in fact do relate to their homes, and whether the home can be a site for writing. Another essay here, "On Writing Short Books," arose after pondering the issue of brevity in relation to publishing. This paper was read at a panel on "short fiction" for the Scandinavian Association of American Studies at their annual conference in Trondheim, Norway, in 2003. This essay also appeared in condensed form in *World Literature Today* in the May-August 2003 issue.

The essay "Poetry and the Idea of Home" was written when I was asked by Dr. Deborah Keahey at the University of Winnipeg to speak to a panel on "Making It Home" at the University of Winnipeg during the Winnipeg Writers' Festival in 2000. At that time I spoke mostly about Don McKay's ideas, but later I expanded the thoughts I had written for the panel into the essay included here. In 2003, I read a shortened version of this essay to students and faculty at the University of Oklahoma in Norman during the Neustadt Jury symposium. The composition of this essay brought home to me the idea that is behind the title of this whole collection, *Stranger at the Door*. For the writer, a need to write simply presents itself: either on a subject or a theme or about an image or to develop an emotion. The process starts, and the writer rarely actually knows where it is going, but finds out only by going there—as Stephen King admonishes, "Why be such a control freak?" (165). The act of composition is therefore often described as an exciting journey. Or one may characterize it, as I have alluded here, as a sudden visit from a stranger. You invite the stranger in and what happens, happens. That could mean anything. Things could go anywhere from there.

In order not to be a "control freak" in writing, the professor and the student as well necessarily have to learn to let go in the writing seminar. Because we give up old systems of domination in that site, ideally (not everyone succeeds at this), the writing seminar is, as Madison Smartt Bell says, profoundly paradoxical. Conflicts, antagonisms, sensitivities, and disagreements come up all the time. bell hooks talks about a "live" classroom in her book *Teaching to Transgress*, and it is very nearly a description of the writing seminar. Although bell hooks isn't referring specifically to a writing education, she could be, because it is "the call for a recognition of cultural diversity, a rethinking of ways of knowing, a deconstruction of old epistemologies, and the concomitant demand that there be a transformation in our classrooms, in how we teach and what we teach" (29-30). Everything is rethought, right down to prejudices and presuppositions and the uses of discourses and meaning of words. The writing seminar does what writers do, which is to engage in "a necessary revolution," in bell hooks' phrase, "one that seeks to restore life to a corrupt and dying academy" (30). What is exciting about the process is precisely that it is "alive," and it is the re-enlivening, or reinvigoration of language and vision that drives the process of learning writing and of writing.

Creative writing exists in an uneasy relationship to criticism because sometimes criticism has no effect on writing and publishing. Two cases in point in recent years have been the phenomena of J.K. Rowling and Paulo Coelho. Nothing critics can (or do) say will alter the fact that readers want to read the books these writers have written. Their books seem to exist on a plane that is immune to anything anyone says. Perhaps at the bottom of such phenomena—and what is at the bottom of writing itself—is a thought voiced by Coelho in an interview he gave with Glauco Ortolano for *World Literature Today* in the spring of 2003. When asked what lies behind his works, and why their success is so stunning (despite the criticisms of literary experts), Coelho points out that he articulates in his writing our ambitions, which, whether we always realize it or not, are to "die alive." This phrase simply means "being aware of and participating in things until the day we die" (58). When pressed further, Coelho notes that "people end up dying to the world on the day they renounce their dreams" (58). We are aware of our desire to be "alive" in that way, and the desire to write is the same thing as having dreams that are vibrant with us. Rather than using all our energy, he says, to keep what is alive in us under control (like a volcano) and thereby destroy what is around us, it is better to let it all explode. To let it go: in other words, to write.

The books I have referred to along the way are books I was reading over the years, and discussing with students as well. I have looked for writers' views from various cultures, from European, African, North American, and Asian. I have simply wanted to hear what writers have to say. Along the way, some of the essayists and writers have become important to me, and I have made discoveries of kindred spirits in the writing world I did not know I had. Of particular importance to me have been the thoughts of Walter Benjamin, Paul Auster, Maurice Blanchot, Italo Calvino, Mario Vargas Llosa, Ben Okri, and Christa Wolf—as well as those who were important to me before: writers like Roland Barthes, Mikhail Bakhtin, André Brink, Albert Camus, Hélène Cixous, Marguerite Duras, bell hooks, and James Tate. Paul Auster is referred to very often throughout these chapters because his essays in *The Art of Hunger* are very dynamic. They are often very short, in fact some of them are simply brief reviews, but it seems like Auster is unable to say the briefest of things without being profound in some way. His views on literature and writers and culture are almost always dead on, and resonate with me. I also bring in Italo Calvino because he positions himself at the cusp of various traditions and is his own thinker. Both of these writers have opinions they have earned and hold authentically. Hélène Cixous has been an inspiration for a long time; not just because she talks about being a woman writing in today's world, but also because she is able to combine rigorous thoughts with creative expression, and the result is sparkling. Similarly, bell hooks is quite an inspiration because she is radical and fully aware of a writer's (and a teacher's) constraints, and the realism that is behind much of her radicalism is gratifying. Ben Okri's essays, referred to several times here, were a discovery when I was teaching in the Writing Practices Program at Capilano College in North Vancouver for a term. I asked students to read Okri's *A Way of Being Free*, and many of them found this to be the most important book they had read about writing. Okri is not afraid of showing the spiritual side of the writing life, as is Annie Dillard in her own quiet way. While readers of this collection of snapshots into the commentaries that circulate in the writing world may not agree with everything I have included, I hope what I have put together will encourage the reader and writer to keep an open mind and give these commentators a chance to let their thoughts sink in.

# 1 | The Art of Solitude

"It is necessary to be alone," Thomas Merton wrote in the first draft of his essay *Day of a Stranger:*

> to be not part of this, to be in the exile of silence, to be in a manner of speaking a political prisoner. No matter where in the world he may be, no matter what may be his power of protest, or his means of expression, the poet finds himself ultimately where I am. Alone, silent, with the obligation of being very careful not to say what he does not mean, not to let himself be persuaded to say merely what another wants him to say, not to say what his own past work has led others to expect him to say. (18-19)

In so many words, Merton collapses the solitary and the poet. To live at one with nature is to be at one with yourself but also to be like a "political prisoner." Those are also the requirements for the poet. There is something profoundly similar in what ascetics and hermits like Merton, and poets like Jacques Dupin, have to say about their needs. One is led to believe, at almost every turn, that the vocation of prayer and meditation and poetry are almost the same. When speaking of the poet Jacques Dupin, for instance, Paul Auster writes in an essay on him which is included in his collection *The Art of Hunger,* that the poet puts everything away, even his clothes, and addresses the world in nakedness.[1] For the poet, "the poem is a kind of spiritual purification" (182). Authenticity and being alive to the present moment are what both the writer and the solitary need. Thomas Merton is certainly not alone in making the connection between solitude and writing. Closer to home, Saskatchewan writer Sharon Butala says something similar in her book *The Perfection of the Morning.* In her essay "Telling the Truth," Butala tells us that the creative process resembles meditation. She writes: "I see myself trying to be still enough and pure and quiet enough that I will become a hollow vessel through which 'the angel'—which I conceive of as the Creative Flow—will speak" (11).

*Notes to chapter 1 are on p. 107.*

The story behind Thomas Merton's essay *Day of a Stranger* (which was published as a small book and included his photographs), is Merton's move to the hermitage in the hills above the Abbey of Gethsemani in Kentucky, where he lived as a monk. He hermitted himself in the summer of 1965, after having wanted to for a long time, and preparing himself for it. Apparently Merton found great happiness in that concrete block of a bungalow with only an outhouse for facilities, insects to fend with, heat and cold to ward off, and no one to talk to. According to Robert E. Daggy, writing from Bellarmine College in 1980, what made Merton love the hermitage most was that "it became the closest thing to a home of his own that Merton had ever known" (9). It was a space where he could unfold, without restrictions, and be his own, true self. When asked by a South American editor to describe a typical day in his hermitage, Merton found himself revising and cutting down his essay, removing its emotional content little by little, until he had emptied the text of all but the most matter-of-fact observations. "This is not a hermitage," he wrote, "it is a house" (41). His essay became anti-mystical, for he found the simple and the real were also the most magical and needed no further comment. The process he describes here is a journey towards silence; even in the act of writing he leans towards the wordless. The story is told of Merton, both in his autobiography, *The Seven Story Mountain*, and in biographies of him, that when he was a young man, he desperately wanted to be a published poet. As he grew older, became a Catholic, and joined the Cistercian order, the need for fame fell away. Yet it was then that his friends began to make trips to visit him and retrieve his writings for publication. It was when he stopped trying that his wishes were fulfilled. Anthony T. Padovano, in his biography *The Human Journey; Thomas Merton: Symbol of a Century*, writes that Merton had discovered "the sense of self-integrity that good writing requires" (47). The writer "found happiness the moment he stopped looking for it," Padovano says.

Franz Kafka is also said to have written as intensely and meaningfully as he did because he had little hope for publishing success. French theorist Hélène Cixous interprets that impossibility of publication as a kind of freedom. She describes her idea of Kafka's final written texts. In her essay "The Last Painting," Cixous speaks of Kafka the dying man who has nothing further to strive for. His (written) phrase is, she says, "a phrase that fell from his hand…at the moment he was not striving to be a writer, the moment he was Franz Kafka himself, beyond books" (*Coming to Writing* 116). She is talking about a note he scribbled on a piece of paper just before he died, and this image speaks of the position of the writer in the act of writing: you can only truly write when you are untied from the moorings of your life and have no ambition except to be in the present moment. Cixous believes the freedom that comes with abandoning ambition gives writing life. In her words, "It's at the end, at the moment when one has attained the period of relinquishing, of adoration, and no longer of gilding, that miracles happen" (117). The operative word here for this discussion is "adoration," where Cixous links writing and prayerful worship. Paul Auster also talks about Kafka in this context. The last weeks and days of Kafka's life confirm to Auster the collapse of the writer and the solitary—even the hermit monk who has abandoned all worldly ambition. In his essay "Kafka's Letters," Auster exclaims that "Kafka's life and art were inseparable: to succeed in his art meant to consume himself as a human being. He wrote, not for recognition, but because his very life depended on it. As he expressed in his diary: 'Writing is a form of prayer'" (135).

It is not necessary, however, to be Thomas Merton, a Trappist monk and sometime hermit, to recognize certain truths about life, the spirit, and language. Even conventional psychotherapy will tell you that in order to be happy, it is not what you add to your life that counts, it is what you take away. Writers have known this on some basic level since writing began: the more you add (money, material objects, obligations, even recognition), the less is left for you to nurture the solitude you need to continue with your writing. Or, if you do continue writing anyway, you may, writers are quick to suspect, not be writing as well; your work may not be as real and as true as it would be if you kept your integrity and freedom. In her book *The Writing Life*, for example, Annie Dillard says unequivocally that "the life of sensation is the life of greed; it requires more and more. The life of the spirit requires less and less, time is ample and its passage sweet" (*Writing* 32-33). Dillard counsels writers to avoid attractive work spaces, and explains how she covers the windows of her work studio and keeps the walls bare so she will not be distracted. The idea of a retreat without distractions is so uniformly considered necessary for writing that places like the St. Peter's Benedictine monastery in Saskatchewan has long set aside retreats for writers among the monks, in the belief that writing and spiritual pursuits are inextricably linked. Such a connection is proposed by the most unlikely proponents. Hugo Ball, for example—an early founder of Dadaism in Europe, who had no connection to anything religious— wrote in a diary entry in 1921, that "the socialist, the aesthete, the

*N.B.*

monk: all three agree that modern bourgeois education must be destroyed" (Auster 61).[2] Ball means that integrity, creativity, and solitude are necessary for the pursuit of the ideal purity of purpose that a "bourgeois" education complicates. Clarity and simplicity come only with the kind of "unlearning" that is found in a life of solitude.

The argument made by these writers is that in order to write authentically, it is necessary to clear the mind and even the space in which the writing takes place. The life behind the writing, as well as the work of writing itself, requires the kind of "purification" these comments allude to. Salman Rushdie says, for example, in his essay "Imaginary Homelands," that "the imagination works best when it is free" (20). It is only when the mind is unencumbered that creative work is possible. It also happens naturally that the writing act in itself clarifies the mind. You think better and more clearly while you are writing. Ben Okri voices similar thoughts in his essays on writing. In his collected essays on writing, *A Way of Being Free*, Okri argues that writing and spiritual grace are fundamentally linked. For example, in "Newton's Child" he claims that

> The highest kind of writing—which must not be confused with the most ambitious kind…belongs to the realm of grace. Talent is part of it, certainly; a thorough understanding of the secret laws, absolutely. But finding the subject and theme which is in perfect harmony with your deepest nature, your forgotten selves, your hidden dreams, and the full unresonated essence of your life—now that cannot be reached through searching, nor can it be stumbled upon through ambition. That sort of serendipity comes upon you on a lucky day. It may emerge even out of misfortune or defeat. You may happen upon it without realising that this is the work through which your whole life will sing. We should always be ready. We should always be humble. Creativity should always be a form of prayer. (26-27)

Okri could hardly be more precise. Writing is akin to prayer, and it is a spiritual pursuit which comes to you the way grace does. It is nothing you can rush. The idea of the work of writing is therefore qualified by other, less tangible factors, of which writers like Rushdie and Okri are fully cognizant.

The notion that writing is sacred has been articulated by many. Hélène Cixous, for whom writing is seen as an extreme form of liberation, both psychologically and politically, discusses the relationship the act of writing has to the sacred. For her, to write was to cut through the debris of received thought and come to something personal and pure. She makes a distinction, though, between the approach taken by men such as those I've referred to here, and her own approach. She sees the "male tradition" as separate: for "the sons of the book," solitude and the symbolic desert were acknowledged features of writing, but their vision of that connection involved a form of elitism which Cixous wishes to distance herself from. Her description of such elitism attempts to explain what writing means to the "male tradition." That is, writing

> asked everything of them, took everything from them, it was merciless and tender, it dispossessed them entirely of all riches, all bonds, it lightened them, stripped them bare; then it granted them passage: toward the most distant, the nameless, the endless. It gave them leave. (*Coming* 14)

Or, put differently, while the writer in that ascetic tradition surrenders entirely to the writing process, he is also empowered by it. There need not be a great discrepancy between what is described as empowerment and what we know of as the long tradition of monasticism. And the distinction between the "male tradition" Cixous speaks of and the view of writing as truly liberating for a woman in a similar manner need not be disjointed. Cixous adjures the [woman] writer: "Let yourself go! Let go of everything! Lose everything!" (40). And, she says "whatever you value, give it up" (40). This advice sounds similar to that of Thomas Merton.

What does Cixous advocate for the serious writer? In her essay on painting, "The Last Painting," she advises that in order to produce art,

> one has to have broken off with everything that holds one back: calculations, backward or sideways glances, hidden motives, acquired, accumulated, hardened knowledge. And especially all the fears: fear of the unknown, fear of criticism, fear of not knowing, fear of the evil eye. (*Coming* 112-13)

She contends that to be an artist in the first place, spiritual, emotional, and physical freedom is necessary. That means it is not possible to write or paint or compose if you are a prisoner of your fears or obligations. As Cixous phrases it, "How could we come all the way from our over-furnished memories and our museums of words to the garden of beginnings and rustlings?" (114). That leap is simply too large. Other women have been aware of the discrepancies posed by a traditional woman's life, where there are invariably obligations to children, home, and family pulling at her, and the life of the writer, who needs space, solitude, and time. Teacher and essayist bell hooks talks about this in her essay "the true writer's home," and tells us that even in the midst of the city and the busy milieu of the marketplace, she has "reclaimed a more reclusive space where the power and passion of writing, simply writing, prevails. In that space I do not obsess about audiences, advances, or critical reviews. I just give my all to the work at hand" (*Remembered* 163). The lure of "audience, advances, or critical reviews" is always there, but the process of overcoming those is part of the writer's task. bell hooks continually emphasizes the importance of solitude for writing. So does Paul Auster. In Auster's essay on Giuseppe Ungaretti, "Innocence and Memory," he writes that the poet Ungaretti tried to free himself from his own mental universe in order to disburden himself of all the things he knew, thought, and felt.[3] Auster says that "Ungaretti's determination to situate himself at the extremes of his own consciousness is paradoxically what allows him to cure himself of the fear of these limits" (126). What we are told Ungaretti goes through does not sound very different from what Cixous counsels for women writers, and what bell hooks claims to do for herself either. So the gender disparity voiced by Cixous does not appear to be as great as she feels it is when it comes to writing and the attempt to clear one's mind and connect to something spiritual as well.

Monasticism, or asceticism, with its concomitant solitude, and the freedom or liberty to abandon oneself to one's imagination and dreams, need not be seen as the same thing. But frequently these are conflated, and one is at the back of the other when writers talk about their personal space. Mario Vargas Llosa, for example, writes in his essay "The Truth of Lies," that fiction writers have to abandon themselves and that "to go out of oneself, to be another, in however illusory a fashion, is a way of becoming less of a slave and experiencing the risks of freedom" (361). Risking freedom by abandoning one's hold on one's life is part of the counsel of solitude. Eudora Welty also speaks to this issue in various ways and contexts, included in her book of essays called *The Eye of the Story*. In an essay on Willa Cather, "The House of Willa Cather," Welty talks about Cather's *The Song of the Lark* and in particular about the character Thea's teacher's admonition there that "every artist makes himself born. It is very much harder than the other time, and longer" (59). Welty points out the advice of Miss Jewett as something to note—that "You must find a quiet place. You must find your own quiet center of life and write from that" (48). In another essay,

"Place in Fiction," Welty is even more direct. Speaking of the ability to focus, she explains that "the act of focusing itself has beauty and meaning" (113). The ability to focus, it would seem, requires some freedom from pressing distractions, and a measure of quiet. Welty says poetically that "as soon as the least of us stands still, that is the moment something extraordinary is seen to be going on in the world" (113). To see the world at all, one might add, it is necessary to stand still; to reach a still point from which the movements and noises of the world can be observed. To write, you need to see the world.[4]

Put another way, or putting another angle on the subject of writing and solitude: it is not what you know that matters, but how you think. It is not quantity of information you need in order to write, it is quality of mind. As in any thoughtful occupation, the road to writing has no shortcuts and there are no magic formulas. You earn your way to a good text; you put in the time, the work, and the inquisitive, tolerant, and even humble, attitude that will transport you there. The distinction between what you know and how you know it is something the fifteen-year-old protagonist Sophie, in Jostein Gaarder's novel *Sophie's World,* discovers.[5] Gaarder wrote his successful novel originally to help  him teach younger students the basic principles of philosophy. Sophie is "every student" who gets letters sent to her regularly with brief lessons in philosophy. Each letter has a few questions to ponder and a lecture on philosophy. Sophie eventually finds philosophy an interesting preoccupation, because with philosophy, unlike school, she does not have to memorize anything. Thinking is not about memorizing:  "She decided that philosophy was not something you can learn," we are told. "But perhaps you can learn to *think* philosophically" (40). This is another way of saying it is more important to take away than to add. To simplify, clarify, cleanse the mind and, consequently life, you re-orient yourself. Perhaps this may simply be seen as a way of being conscious: to live in accordance with what you know, rather than separating your knowledge into a compartment that does not have to touch your daily life. Perhaps if we all acted on what we know, we would all be doing very different things. Knowledge, when it is real, needs to be internalized, which seems to be young Sophie's discovery.

Christa Wolf has also discussed the nature of the "heightened" mental life that comes with writing, which aligns writing with a certain form of spirituality as well.[6] Wolf, who is originally from East Germany and whose writing has been politically charged, is otherwise a very secular writer. Her experience, however, has made her think that writers, by virtue of their occupation and what is required of them, are different from what she calls "normal" people. In a conversation about her book *A Model Childhood*, she says that

> being a writer does leave its mark. There are moments and periods of heightened calm in which you reflect on your experiences. You have a sense of viewing things differently, even when they are happening, from how you would have had you not been a writer. This is a remarkable thing. It is simply a fact that if you write, even if it is only one book every ten years, yet see yourself the whole time as a writer, then you live differently from how you would if you just lived normally.... Your powers of observation are heightened, you feel a continual pressure of responsibility, a constant commitment. All these feelings are incredibly strong and come down to the fact that, whether you like it or not, you are there to describe your experiences.... It is immaterial whether you are very good or not really all that good. The simple fact that you know you are there to describe your experience, makes a great difference. (58)

Wolf is talking about a state of heightened consciousness—and also a sense of alienation—that comes with the writing process.

Some heightening of consciousness, to use the same phrase, is clearly desirable in society as a whole. But what these writers are talking about is perhaps more intense, more poetic and spiritual, than the idea of being fully aware of what is around you—the way anyone might try to be aware. However the difference is only one of degree, not of quality. At least one can expect people to reach for such a state—and they do, if the popularity of authors like Coelho and Gaarder is any indication. Both writers have produced works that encourage the quest for learning and self-awareness. And society needs such encouragement, or it will not be able to function. That is a position argued by John Ralston Saul in his book *The Unconscious Civilization*. For Saul, it is not so much a spiritual matter as it is social, political, and even economic. Unless we are conscious, he maintains, we cannot act intelligently. What he does not point out is how hard it is to integrate thought and feeling, action and knowledge. It simply is not easy, and Saul sets the bar high. Writers tend to be clearer on the process involved. But Saul articulates the matter in his own way when he maintains that "the true characteristic of consciousness is...not simply knowledge, but a balanced use of our qualities so that what we know and say is related to what we do" (186). To illustrate this point, he uses the example of Thomas Jefferson, who said that everything in life depends on how you approach reality. When handled in the right way, the right frame of mind, and in the right spirit, the "Gordian knot" of all the things in life that are unexplainable will untie itself effortlessly (192).

It has always seemed to me that good accomplishments are unlikely unless the life they come out of is good. It seems like it would be very difficult to have a complex and frustrated home life which the writer then turns around and switches off in order to work. It is hard to think when conditions are adverse. Many writers have apparently done so, but the conditions that will empower good work must be there. In order to write well, I believe it is necessary to live well. As Annie Dillard says: "There is no shortage of good days. It is good lives that are hard to come by" (*Writing* 32). We know this instinctively, and this is what attracts us to good writing. The mind behind the words reveals itself. In *The Writing Life*, Dillard asks the question most often pondered by practitioners of imaginative writing: "How do you prepare yourself, all alone, to enter an extraordinary state on an ordinary morning?" (47). The right mood, atmosphere, tone, all have to be found. About her own experience, Dillard confesses that "I could not add a word until I was ready, or that word would enfeeble or punctuate the work" (48).

Laura Riding, the American poet who was perhaps most famous for her association with Robert Graves, expresses such sentiments as well in her unusual text *The Telling*.[7] Her comment on the relationship between the writer and her text is quoted in an essay on her by Paul Auster, titled "Truth, Beauty, Silence." Here Riding remarks that "if what you write is true, it will not be so because of what you are as a writer but because of what you are as a being. There can be no literary equivalent to truth. If, in writing, truth is the quality of what is said, told, this is not a literary achievement: it is a simple human achievement" (Auster, 73). Paul Auster, who admires Riding's work, adds the observation that Riding's view of life and writing is similar to Ben Jonson's, who once claimed that "only a good man is capable of writing a good poem." Auster notes that this connection between the work and the person "is an idea that stands at one extreme of our literary consciousness, and it places poetry within an essentially moral framework" (73-74).

When Italo Calvino was asked to deliver the Charles Norton lectures at Harvard in 1984, which were later published as *Six Memos for the Next Millennium*, he tried to find six or eight essential elements of the writing act that would fix the spirit of the practice for him. He finally decided on five (there were more, but he could not finish them):

lightness; quickness; exactitude; visibility; and multiplicity. He wanted
to approach the delicacy and heightened sensibility that accompanies
writing when it is real and authentic. Lightness was for him a quality
that involved spiritualizing the world through writing. The world as we
know it is heavy with itself, he infers. History goes into negative spi-
rals and entraps us. Life itself entraps us. He talks about "the weight,
the inertia, the opacity of the world—qualities that stick to writing
from the start, unless one finds some way of evading them" (4). This
is a remarkable insight into writing, and emphasizes the way in which
the writer is thinking rather than broad and hard issues of "craft."
Calvino goes on to confess that "I felt that the entire world was turning into stone: a slow petrification" (4). When the sheer weight of existence is bearing down so hard on a person, it is difficult to imagine
how creative activity can emanate. This notion of lightness as a quality a writer needs in order to work is much the same as Christa Wolf's
call for "poise." Christa Wolf's words are: "we should aim for lightness
and poise in the treatment of our material" (11). Writers everywhere seem
to have made comments that are in agreement with Calvino's sense of
the five qualities he writes about in *Six Memos*—especially this quality of lightness. Even highly politicized writers like André Brink, when
speaking most politically, talks about the necessity for a personal and
linguistic "lightening" in the writer's attitude. Brink's book *Writing in
a State of Siege* is a collection of essays on the subject of being a white
writer in South Africa during apartheid. Brink finds the world he is
living in understandably heavy and believes it can be transformed and
enlightened by the writer's imagination. As such, the very qualities
needed for good imaginative writing are also qualities needed to reform
society itself.[8] The writer, he claims, has to transform himself in order
to be worthy of the occupation of writing at all.

When Calvino speaks about lightness, he explains by saying "I
mean that I have to change my approach, look at the world from a different perspective, with a different logic and with fresh methods of
cognition and verification" (7). To change yourself from the inside is
a precursor to changing your language. The expansive range of fiction
itself needs an unfettered mind to express it. All of these qualities are
present in discussions on writing penned by very political and socially
oriented writers, whose lives depend on the truth of what they are
saying. Chinua Achebe, for example, writing about the lives of Nigerians
in times of huge cultural and social transition, says in his book *Hopes
and Impediments* that these concerns follow him into a life of dislo-

cation in the United States. Achebe argues in his essay "The Truth of Fiction" that "fiction calls into full life our total range of imaginative faculties and gives us a heightened sense of our personal, social and human reality" (151). Christa Wolf, Italo Calvino, André Brink, Chinua Achebe: as different as they are, they know the need for a kind of inner lightness, freedom of thinking, release from convention and habit, and purity of thought.

These writers are voicing in a secular way what Thomas Merton found in his Trappist monastery: that we are deceived by what we think of as our phenomenal reality. It is the life of the mind and spirit which is more real, and this heightened reality can be found only by casting off the baggage of the world you are in. In Italo Calvino's words, this is a kind of wisdom that is necessary for a writer to have. He claims in this context that "what many consider to be the vitality of the times—noisy, aggressive, revving and roaring—belongs to the realm of death, like a cemetery for rusty old cars" (12). It is this vision that makes the marketplace so damaging for artists, for they have to take their hard-won, spiritual wares to the court of commerce and flog them, and themselves, like clowns. Such thinking—which pits the artist in his solitude against the chaos and noise of the world, has a long and venerated tradition. The idea comes up in one of the earliest modernist novels of the twentieth century: James Joyce's *A Portrait of the Artist as a Young Man.* This novel is about the development of a writer, and we see how the principal character, Stephen Dedalus, matures to become the artist he wishes to be. At the centre of his self-discovery lies the realization that he has to separate himself from the busy world. He cannot find inspiration in the middle of chaos. In the narrator's words, Stephen realizes that "to merge his life in the common tide of other lives was harder for him than any fasting or prayer" (164).

In *Six Memos,* Calvino focuses on what I think is the most important aspect concerning writing and simplicity. The writer has to begin all over; to deconstruct language and image and reality until the smallest available unit is found, and then start to construct again from a clean slate.[9] The fact is that language becomes tainted with usage. People use words carelessly. Advertising manipulates the meaning of words. Images fall on us from everywhere, dissociating us from our knowledge and experience. The writer should not, must not, add to this confusion. The writer sorts it out instead. Calvino's way of saying this is, "It seems to me that language is always used in a random, approximate, careless manner, and this distresses me unbearably" (56).

What should be the tool to wisdom, namely language, becomes the weapon of confusion. For Calvino, literature is "the Promised Land in which language becomes what it really ought to be" (56). He puts this distressing concern in a more dramatic way when he declares that

> a pestilence has struck the human race in its most distinctive faculty—that is, the use of words. It is a plague afflicting language, revealing itself as a loss of cognition and immediacy, an automatism that tends to level out all expression into the most generic, anonymous, and abstract formulas, to dilute meanings, to blunt the edge of expressiveness, extinguishing the spark that shoots out from the collision of words and new circumstances. (56)

The same, he says, is true for images. "We live in a rainfall of images" (57) he writes, and the carelessness and randomness of the plethora of images around us leads to alienation and distress. Therefore, exactitude and authenticity of thought, extreme care, and delicacy are required for the writing act. Good writing, in so many words, requires good thinking. Not quantity, which the advent of the computer has doubtlessly aided in bringing about, but quality. The method of pen and ink, which made writing more laborious, also gave the writer more time to think. As Calvino sees it, "We are bombarded today by such a quantity of images that we can no longer distinguish direct experience from what we have seen for a few seconds on television. The memory is littered with bits and pieces of images, like a rubbish dump" (92).

For so many writers, the sanctity of the imaginative act is crucial. In his essay "The Truth of Fiction," for instance, Chinua Achebe declares that "the life of the imagination is a vital element of our total nature. If we starve it or pollute it the quality of our life is depressed or soiled" (*Hopes* 147). It is, in other words, crucial for the writer to keep her mind clear and unpolluted by the confusion that encircles us. Witness John Ralston Saul, who claims in *The Unconscious Civilization* that the writer is more necessary today—as a force for social change—than at any other time. Saul complains that "there have been so many writers, so many books, such a babble of language flowing around us via so many new communication devices. And more language-distributing technology arrives in the public place every day" (44). The landscape of ideas has become so murky, and it is the writer's task to clarify at least some of it. Both Achebe and Saul sound here like purists, and their argument is quite spiritual in nature. It sounds like writing is close to prayer, and further, to meditation. Even the most secular writers, who do not profess any sort of spiritual bent, will find themselves speaking of writing as prayer. There is, in most people's experience, a devotional aspect to creating art, which is akin to the experience of purgation offered by prayer, confession, and the saying of mantras. Hélène Cixous, for example, in speaking of the painter Claude Monet, talks about painting canvases as a journey through the stations of the cross: the painter stops at each station when he produces a canvas. She notes that "Seen by us, these canvases were 'beautiful.' Seen by him they are obstacles on the path to the last one" (129). Such comments may sound more mystical than they are, but Cixous's statements need not be seen as mystical at all. She talks about "sunflower life" in the same way Thomas Merton talks about seeing the world as it essentially is, and finding the sacred there, in the world itself. Cixous uses the image of the sunflower because of Van Gogh's famous impressionist painting of the sunflower: the flower is painted as it is, in itself, and the artist is the one who sees the world clearly.

Poet and essayist Tim Lilburn takes the idea of the connection between poetry and the mystical further than most, while still speaking secularly. His arguments may serve as a further fine-tuning of what is being laid out by all these other writers concerning language, thought, and the written word in today's world. Lilburn has written on the subject of the contemplative as poet, in much the same way Thomas Merton has. Even though Lilburn's perspective is secular, he freely uses the image or trope of the medieval monk and relies on Christian scripture to elucidate what is going on when a poet writes a poem. In his essay "How to Be Here?" which is included in his collection *Poetry and Knowing*, Lilburn talks about how the poet needs to use knowledge, science, and sensitivity in the quest for a poem. Like Van Gogh, Lilburn advises going out into the landscape and looking at the essential stone, essential tree: looking at things as they are, without interpretation and personality. He comes to the idea of "unknowing" as a way for the poet to shed himself in the act of discovering something essential in the world. When the poet is alone in the landscape, like Merton, Lilburn says "This is a good place to take one's time in, watch, crane into the distance of things.... This is a good place to learn sorrow, *luctus*, what the old monks called *penthos*, a bleak place to enact a politics of silence and solitude" (167). Later he reiterates the necessity of losing language itself—paradoxical though it may sound—and abandoning the names of things. He writes, with specific reference to the landscape of Saskatchewan, where the prairie is vast and silent, and therefore inspiring for a poet: "This is a land to wait in, watching. Bring anonymity; namelessness has a place here; the land worn to the bone hints into you an interior mimesis of namelessness. Bring sorrow. Watch" (167).

As Lilburn's argument goes on, he collapses the contemplative and the poet, and the whole idea of mysticism becomes part of the ordinary resources of the poet. His is an extreme position, but hardly more so than the notions proposed by Hélène Cixous. Using the terms *poet* and *contemplative* or *monk* almost interchangeably, Lilburn notes that "The monk is poured into waiting, watching and tears" (168) the same way the poet is. What the poet needs to know is both everything and nothing. For him, "contemplation grows out of the wreckage of other forms of knowing, other forms of being," and contemplation is, in fact, "in part, their wreckage" (168). In his own language, Lilburn is echoing the notion that in order to find yourself, you must lose yourself, which is a central Christian precept. He claims that:

> the impulse to know the world contemplatively ends in asceticism, that knowing can be this renunciation of self, that the pursuit of ascetical virtue and knowledge are coterminous. The desire to know the world behind its names is the death of knowing which is objective, ordering, communicable and the apparently secure life that rests on such knowing. (168)

In essence he is arguing that the poet as well as the contemplative discovers that the search for knowledge ends in the absence of objective knowing, which he calls "unknowing," echoing the medieval treatment of the same theme found in *The Cloud of Unknowing*. There are different forms of knowing involved, Lilburn implies, and says that "the physical world cannot be known in the way poetry aspires to know it, intimately, ecstatically, in a way that heals the ache of one's separation from the world" (169). We see him coming full circle from leaving the world to desiring the world and being essentially unable to appropriate the world and still write.

The hard-won insights into the relationship between thinking, writing, and being alone, which Thomas Merton explicates by his life and writings and by the interviews he gave, have been echoed and maintained by other, very secular, writers as well. People who have been forced to be alone, such as people in exile, refugees, the ostracized from social and political milieus, have often become acutely aware of the clarity that comes with solitude. To illustrate this more secular example, there is an interview from 1978 which Paul Auster conducted with Edmond Jabès.[10] Jabès was exiled from Egypt, where he had lived all his life, after the advent of World War II, because he was a Jew. He went to Paris with his family and wrote, among other things, *The Book of Questions*. In this interview, published as "Providence," Jabès talks about various aspects of being alone, without a country, without roots, and how he has attached his idea of nation and belonging to books. It is crystal clear to Edmond Jabès that writing involves risk-taking, simply because the writer has undergone the process of unlearning and is prepared to see things afresh. He claims that "if there is no risk, there is no writing" (145). For that clarity to emerge, though, he maintains there is a necessity for solitude as well: "the risks a writer takes must be taken alone" (145) he calls it.

To round off these disparate observations on the relationship between writing and solitude, there is an essay by Marguerite Duras that is simply called "Writing," and which expresses many of the ideas and thoughts raised here and which are present in Thomas Merton's essay *Day of a Stranger*.[11] Yet the two writers approach the subject of solitude from opposite angles. It seems that no matter where writers come from, they end up with the same reality. Duras's essay is about her house in Neauphle, which she bought with the funds earned from a film. This house became her "hermitage," where she could contemplate, dream, be alone, and write. She remarks on the necessity of such a place— that "the solitude of writing is a solitude without which writing could not be produced, or would crumble, drained bloodless by the search for something else to write" (2). Her attitude to writing is that instead of running around looking for things to write about, she needs to stay in one place, be silent and alone, and then her books will come to her. "The person who writes books must always be enveloped by a separation from others," she claims (3). However, inside the solitude Duras is talking about is the reality of doubt. Doubt, all kinds of doubt, is central to writing. For Duras, "it's a practical state in which one can be lost and unable to write anymore.... As soon as one is lost with nothing left to write, to lose, one writes" (9). She is talking about the fundamental doubt a writer has of not being able to write. Perhaps the state of mind she is looking for is the humility that is required of the monk and the solitary as well. But for Duras, the silence she has in mind is more like "being alone in a shelter during the war" (15). Here the image is made as stark as it could be: the cacophony and violence of the world, lamented by Italo Calvino, can be countered by the writer who is, like Sharon Butala has said, willing to be simple and still.

# 2 | The Diasporic Imagination
## Writers' Perspectives

Mario Vargas Llosa, the Peruvian writer known for having once run for the presidency of Peru, and for having been president of PEN, once wrote an essay on what it was like to write his novel *The Green House*.[1] He was living in Paris at the time, but his novel was to take place in the Amazon, the place of his origins. He had to retrace his incomplete memory of things, and ended up having to find books in the Paris library on Amazonian trees. He had to study up on the natives of his own native landscape. But he was somehow compelled, emotionally, to write this book, which had no relation to the place in which he was living at the time. His sense of emotional dislocation is expressed in a well-chosen metaphor. He describes how he went, now and again, to the zoo at the Bois de Vincennes to look at the jungle animals. Then, he tells us in his book *A Writer's Reality*, "every time I saw a puma or a vicuna, I remember what another Peruvian writer who had also lived in Paris many years wrote. This writer, Ventura Garcia Calderon, commented that when he would pass by the llama's cage, the animal's eyes would fill with tears of sadness upon recognizing a compatriot" (77-78). Both of these Peruvians were, at those times, diasporic writers: caught between the past and the present, between reality and the imagination, and empowered emotionally by the dislocation.[2]

The notion of diaspora originally referred to the dispersion of the Jews, and to Jewish Christians living outside Palestine. *Webster's Dictionary* defines diaspora in those terms, and its Greek etymology has to do with scattering and sowing. It is a word rich with implication, and is now used for any scattered nation that lives outside its original homeland, whether it is a racially or ideologically or religiously determined nation. But it serves us well to focus back on the original use of the term when exploring what it means to be a diasporic writer today: that is, a writer living away from her homeland and perhaps writing in a foreign language, but for whom the original tribe or place or home contains the site of her imagination. She writes about a place in which she is not living and in a language not spoken there. The contention here will be, as Canadian expatriate writer Nancy Huston remarks in an interview in the *Globe and Mail*, "Expatriates learn a lot about the human condition that most people aren't aware of. The specificity of childhood, for example."[3]

The dilemmas and conflicts and contradictions imposed on the diasporic writer were elucidated at length early on by Jewish writers in Europe. Hannah Arendt highlights the situation of the diasporic writer in her discussion of Franz Kafka and Walter Benjamin, in her introduction to Benjamin's collection of essays titled *Illuminations*. Arendt quotes from a letter Kafka wrote to Max Brod about German-Jewish writers. As a Jew in Prague during the early part of the century, Franz Kafka is said to have somehow prophesied the Holocaust by some of the images that appeared in his fiction, such as "The Hunger Artist," long before these things ever happened. The subject of his letter to his friend Brod is the so-called "Jewish question." Here is Arendt's summary of Kafka's exposition:

> In a letter to Max Brod about German-Jewish writers he [Kafka] said that the Jewish question or "the despair over it was their inspiration— an inspiration as respectable as any other but fraught, upon closer examination, with distressing peculiarities. For one thing, what their despair discharged itself in could not be German literature which on the surface it appeared to be," because the problem was not really a German one. Thus they lived "among three impossi- bilities...: the impossibility of not writing" as they could get rid of their inspiration only by writing; "the impossibility of writing in German"...and finally, "the impossibility of writing differently," since no other language was available. "One could almost add a fourth impossibility," says Kafka in conclusion, "the impossibility of writing, for this despair was not something that could be mitigated through writing." (31)

Kafka's list of contradictions covers a wide territory. What faces the writer in diaspora almost inevitably involves the kind of "despair" he mentions. The despair of dislocation on many levels acts as the source of inspiration for the artist, but it is a peculiar inspiration. The writer downloads into the culture he lives among the concepts of another culture. This makes writing almost impossible, so the writer cannot fully release that inspiration. If he does write, he has the problem of the language in which he writes, which is not his own and not an appropriate vehicle. Nor can the writer actually write, for whatever inspires him is not unloaded, so to speak. This list is only the beginning. As it happens, Kafka published very little during his lifetime. Neither did Walter Benjamin, a German-Jew living in Paris during the second World War. Both writers are now, however, regarded as path-breaking geniuses in their respective genres, and it is clear to critics that their diasporic condition enhanced their uniqueness and insight.

One such case in point is the mid-century poet Paul Celan.[4] His story is perhaps emblematic of the diasporic writer's condition, writ large. Paul Auster, in an essay titled "The Poetry of Exile," describes the situation in which Celan found himself through no fault of his own. Celan was "a Jew, born in Romania, who wrote in German and lived in France" (90). Added to this geographic and linguistic dislocation is the emotional dislocation of the second World War. Celan was a "victim of the Second World War, survivor of the death camps," and committed "suicide before he was fifty." Says Auster, "Paul Celan was a poet of exile, an outsider even to the language of his own poems, and…his life was exemplary in its pain, a paradigm of the destruction and dislocation of mid-century Europe" (90). It is possible to see Paul Celan as an example of the prototypical twentieth-century writer, for whom dislocation and the pain that multilayered homelessness entails is fundamental. In fact, Celan wrote about his sufferings during the Holocaust almost exclusively, "and his poems are everywhere informed by its memory" (91), Auster notes.

In his essay "Mapmakers," André Brink tells the story of Maxim Gorky's *The Lower Depths*, wherein a poor man in Siberia keeps himself alive by telling himself there is another, better world.[5] The "Virtuous Land" is waiting for him if he can but endure in this life. When a scientist comes with maps and tools and proves to the poor man that there is no such thing in reality as that imaginary land, the poor man goes home and hangs himself. Brink's point with the story is that the writer acts differently. The writer, he says, "turns to his own paper and draws, himself, the map of the Land of Truth he knows exists in himself" (169). It is the same impulse that is attributed to Jorge Luis Borges, who, according to Vargas Llosa, rejected the reality he was faced with in favour of the one he imagined: "The real world was something unacceptable to him and he created this other world, where there are only ideas, knowledge, curiosities that deal with the intellect" (*Writers* 92). Vargas Llosa goes so far as to assert that "fiction is indispensable for mankind, even for people who have never read a book or who are not interested in literature" (149).

Even though André Brink does not appear to be suggesting with his story of the Siberian that writers are just dreamers, he does show the value of pure imagination. When the writer's perceptions interact with the reader's, new ideas may grow. Brink maintains that "what he [the writer] does is to perceive, below the lines of the map he draws, the contours of another world, somehow a more 'essential' world" (169). Brink has been concerned with the issue of the imagination as it relates to politics for most of his career. As a white South African, he has been caught in the juncture of what amounts to cultural civil war. Being a member of a culture he does not wish to defend renders him a spokesman for a culture he may not be seen as belonging to. Brink's condition as a writer involves a peculiar combination of internal diaspora which has given him special insights into the issue of exilic writing and, in particular, the junctures inside which cultures interact. Brink shares these issues with his colleague and fellow South African writer, J.M. Coetzee.

Less politically intended, but equally forceful in terms of the imagination in the social and historical life of a community, is Mario Vargas Llosa's essay "The Truth of Lies" which appears in his book *Making Waves*. Vargas Llosa frequently mentions the relationship between modern Peru and the ancient civilizations of the Incas and Aztecs. Peru, like other South American countries, is perched between the modern world and a sense of something very ancient, which rests in nature. Because much of the history of that more ancient world is unrecorded, it falls on present-day writers to uncover that which is hidden. Vargas Llosa tries to explain the imaginative writer's relationship to historical truth and factual accuracy in relation to his own search for avenues in which to create records in literature that will last. His argument is that writers cannot and should not be held up to accuracy tests, simply because that is a waste of time. History itself is a fiction, and the fiction writer is simply more above-board. He explains the juncture of modern and ancient in relation to writing in an essay titled "Novels Disguised as History," which is included in *A Writer's Reality*. In this essay, Vargas Llosa exclaims that Peru is a juxtaposition of ancient and modern, Native and European: "Two cultures, one Western and modern, the other aboriginal and archaic, hardly coexist, separated from one another because of the exploitation and discrimination that the former exercises over the latter. Our country, our countries, are in a deep sense more a fiction than a reality" (34).

The essay "The Truth of Lies" argues, essentially, that the life of the mind and the imagination turns out to be truer and more psychologically and emotionally accurate than factual reporting could ever be. "One does not write novels to recount life," he writes, "but rather to transform it" (357). Part of the reason for this transformation of life is the simple fact of the screen of language. "Facts suffer a profound change when they are transformed into words," he says ("Truth" 358). It cannot be otherwise. "Because it is not the story which in essence decides the truth of lies of a work of fiction, but the fact that this story is written rather than lived, that it is made of words and not concrete experiences" (358). Truth and lies are, in his view, purely aesthetic terms (359). This is the same process that John Gardner, controversial American author and teacher of writing, talks about in relation to the Heisenberg principle in his book *The Art of Fiction*.[6] The Heisenberg principle asks "to what extent does the instrument of discovery change the discovery, whether the instrument be 'the process of fiction' or the particle bombardment of an atom"? (130). The process for writers is the same as for composers. Once a framework, a tonality, has been decided upon, the creator moulds his thinking to the framework that is there. In Gardner's words, "composers themselves have often expressed the opinion that having first chosen the musical form, one then bends one's thoughts to it" (130). The act of writing, the language and style chosen, takes over.

Vargas Llosa goes so far as to assert that "literature is the realm of ambiguity par excellence. Its truths are always subjective, half-truths which are often flagrant inaccuracies or historical lies" ("Truth" 361). In an earlier essay, "On Being Nine and First Seeing the Sea," Vargas Llosa asserts bluntly that "when you write a novel you must not shrink from the idea of distorting or manipulating reality…because literature…must become a sovereign world" (*Writer's* 79-80). John Gardner makes similar subjective claims concerning "truth" when he asserts that the writer wishes to "'tell the truth'; that is, to get the feeling down in concrete details" (37). Gardner counsels, in fact, that there are three kinds of truths for the writer:

> Telling the truth in fiction can mean one of three things: saying that which is factually correct, a trivial kind of truth, though a kind central to works of verisimilitude; saying that which, by virtue of tone and coherence, does not feel like lying, a more important kind of truth; and discovering and affirming moral truth about human existence—the highest truth of all. (129)

The last two kinds of truth are not the accuracies we associate with so-called "faction" (faction is a term often used for fiction that is based on historical facts and does not manipulate them much), but could be arrived at in various ways, whether literal, symbolic, or figurative.

Jorge Luis Borges argues much the same thing as Vargas Llosa in an essay on "Poetry," published in his collection of lectures called *Seven Nights*. Borges speaks of the poetic as an aesthetic event, and "the aesthetic event is something as evident, as immediate, as indefinable as love, the taste of fruit, of water" (81). Discussing a sonnet by Quevedo, he emphasizes the absurdity of some of the poetic lines in terms of realism.[7] Soldiers weep so much there is a deluge, for example. But he admits to being deeply moved by lines that are, "nonetheless, basically false" (85). You cannot ask of imaginative writing that it be realistic or make sense according to traditional logic. What may be absurd under normal circumstances, "is not absurd in poetry, which has its own laws" (85). The idea that written works can be judged only by their own laws, which when applied to poetry is generally understood and accepted, should be accorded to fiction as well.

So often writers in diaspora are accused of having missed the facts, and instead related some notion from their fantasy and paraded that as historical. But such reading can be simply erroneous. Very often, as Vargas Llosa argues here, the imaginative writer is voicing the imaginative life of the community, and there are sharper truths underlying the narrative than can be taken away from the writer. Since fiction and poetry voice the desires and fears of people in a community, those texts may be controversial, dangerous, attractive, or any number of other things—but not necessarily accurate historically. He asserts that "fiction completes we mutilated beings that have had imposed on us the terrible dichotomy of having only one life and the desires and fantasies to desire one thousand lives. This space between our real life and the desires and fantasies that demand that it be richer and more diverse is the terrain of fiction" ("Truth" 360). On the same note, Eudora Welty, whose essays and reviews were collected in 1983 under the title *The Eye of the Story*, also claims that the realm of fiction is really the emotional world, which may or may not have anything to do with the so-called "real" world. In Welty's words, the writer's past is "in his point of view; his novel, whatever its subject, is the history of his life's experience in feeling" (142).

This more "essential" world need not be simply a fantasy, as it is for the poor Siberian in Gorky's story. The same configurations of reality versus the imagination occur for diasporic writers. Except the writer may hold a truer, or just as true a vision of the "homeland" in his exile as does the one still living in the "old" country. This juncture of realism and truth is much spoken of in diasporic theory and criticism, and the diasporic writer is endlessly challenged on the subject of his own knowledge of the land of his imagination. One of the most vocal and famous of such cases is Salman Rushdie, originally from India but who has lived long in Great Britain, and then in New York, and whose experience of coming under a fatwa for having insulted Islam in *The Satanic Verses* set off an international incident. Rushdie has written perceptively on the problem of what it means to be an exilic or diasporic writer, caught between East and West. In his essay "Imaginary Homelands," Rushdie manages to cover a whole host of concerns about this issue in a few pages.

Rushdie responds to L.P. Hartley's phrase from *The Go-Between* that "the past is a foreign country. They do things differently there."[8] Yet Rushdie inverts the saying, and explains how he sees the present as a foreign country, and "the past is home, albeit a lost home in a lost city in the mists of lost time" (9). He says he has been away from India for so long that he almost regards himself as a foreigner. This does not stop him from writing about India, even though he realizes he will be creating fictions of his own about India: "Indias of the mind" (10). The thing to remember about such imaginary homelands, however, is that while the diasporic writer is creating only a version of the homeland, that version is no more and no less than anyone else's. It is "no more than one version of all the hundreds of millions of possible versions" (10). The question is about memory and its relation to truth, and no one person has a monopoly on that. One reason for the uncertainty of individual memory is that "the past is a country from which we have all emigrated" (12). Everyone is in a state of diaspora from the past and from history. Everyone has a right to draw on his heritage and his own past. Witnesses to this fact abound, as, for example, Günter Grass, James Joyce, Isaac Bashevis Singer, Maxine Hong Kingston, and Milan Kundera.

As Eudora Welty says in her essay "Place in Fiction," "art is never the voice of a country; it is an even more precious thing, the voice of the individual" (117). She argues, in apparent contrast to Mario Vargas Llosa, that the writer is searching for "truth," and truth is individual. The idea that it is possible to find "truth" is not necessarily in opposition to the notion that everything is either fiction, history, or biography, for example, and fiction lies. The difference is about subjective versus objective truth. Emotional truth is not the same as historical truth, and the writer reaches into the underlying realities. In this sense, Rushdie's "India of the mind" is more real than officially recorded historical India or political India. The "truth" is the personal one. It is the public "truth" that lies. There may be more at work here on the psychological and emotional level than the search for a personal truth through the uses of memory, as well. Welty mentions one quite poetic, but probably very real, aspect of memory for the diasporic writer. She says of Marcel Proust, whose great work *Remembrance of Things Past* is a recounting in great detail of the life he has lived, that Proust had discovered "a way of making time give back all it has taken, through turning life by way of memory into art" (172).

The concerns of diasporic writing are more complicated for Chinua Achebe since, as a Nigerian resident in the United States, he writes for a Nigerian audience in English, a language not indigenous to his home country and which is spoken by only a minority there. These facts do not in any way preclude our reception of Achebe as a Nigerian novelist. He has written many essays on the subject of writing in exile, and covers a number of important issues. Achebe also, like Brink, elevates the imaginary over the supposedly real, and discusses fiction writing as inherently unable to pretend to be universal and objective, since nothing can be. Therefore fiction is in many ways truer than so-called non-fiction. He says in his essay "The Truth of Fiction," that "art is man's constant effort to create for himself a different order of reality from that which is given to him; an aspiration to provide himself with a second handle on existence *through his imagination*" (139). Fiction offers us the opportunity to "experience *directly* the highway on which we are embarked and also, *vicariously*, 'the road not taken,' as Robert Frost says" (145).

The idea is that the imagination has equal value to so-called reality. There is spiritual, social, political, and cultural value to shared imaginary "worlds" and blueprints for alternatives to what is far too often a tortuous reality. The perception that imaginary writing has an impact on the practical world has not left the world's regimes idle. André Brink mentions, in this regard, in his essay "The Writer in a State of Siege," the fate of German intellectuals and writers during the Third Reich. He mentions the burning of the Reichstag and that the *autos-da-fé*, arrests, and persecutions, came about because Hitler blamed the intellectuals for what had happened. The result was a "mass exodus of leading writers" who organized a literature-in-exile in other countries (182).

Brink quotes Thomas Mann, who claimed in 1937 that "wherever I am, Germany is" (183).

There is also an obverse condition which relates to the emigration of writers from an oppressive regime that will not let them speak out. This is what has been called "inner emigration," a term that comes up in the context of Christa Wolf. Wolf was an East German writer who wrote under the umbrella of an oppressive socialist regime. She has been accused of complying with the Stasi and her position towards the international intellectual community became tainted as a result. But for her, the idea of "inner emigration" has special significance. She has discussed the fate of those artists who remained in Germany during the Third Reich but did not support it. Instead of leaving the country, they resorted to a "withdrawal into private life" (51, translator's note). In such a case, the artist's private life is more fundamental, more necessary, and real than the official life of the community. Conversely, Salman Rushdie mentions "internal emigration" as a deplorable alternative to active diasporic participation in the cultural lives of the world. "To forget that there is a world beyond the community to which we belong," Rushdie writes, "to confine ourselves within narrowly defined cultural frontiers, would be, I believe, to go voluntarily into that form of internal exile which in South Africa is called the 'homeland'" (19).[9]

The elevation of the imaginary over the practical need therefore not be seen as a bad thing. In other words, the diasporic writer, who is away from home physically but maintains an image of her home imaginatively, and writes out of that imaginary space, need not be viewed as somehow impaired. It is not always a drawback or a hindrance to be dislocated in that way In fact, essayist Annie Dillard, known for her books on living the writer's life, makes a point of counselling writers to deliberately distance themselves from the surroundings of their subjects and rely instead on the imagination. "Write about winter in the summer," she says in *The Writing Life*. "Describe Norway as Ibsen did, from a desk in Italy; describe Dublin as James Joyce did, from a desk in Paris. Willa Cather wrote her prairie novels in New York City; Mark Twain wrote *Huckleberry Finn* in Hartford, Connecticut" (*Writing* 68). You might go so far as to say, along with Salman Rushdie, that the diasporic writer has an advantage over the writer who still lives in his original home community. You could argue that it is the writer at home who is impaired. His vision, his experience, is limited, and writers need a bigger universe. Rushdie mentions an image from Saul Bellow's novel *The Dean's December* to illustrate what he means. In this novel, the central character, listening to a dog bark, "imagines that the barking is the dog's protest against the limit of dog experience" (21). In the same way, writers do not benefit from a limit to the life experience they need to draw from in order to create convincing fictions.

The need to create distance and dislocation even when it is not forced on the writer is spoken of at length by Paul Auster as well. In his discussion of Edmond Jabès, Auster speaks of pushing language, knowledge, and memory "to the limit." He writes, with special reference to Jewish diasporic writers, that "if language is to be pushed to the limit, then the writer must condemn himself to an exile of doubt, to a desert of uncertainty. What he must do, in effect, is create a poetics of absence" (114). In order to write at all meaningfully, in fact, the writer is in a perpetual struggle against the forces of ethnocentrism, cultural smugness, linguistic superficiality, and conceptual and moral narrow-mindedness, all of which are represented by the image of the dog barking to "protest against the limit of dog experience."

It is ethnocentrism and its resultant moral smugness that become deadly to creativity. For this reason, Jewish intellectuals in Europe between the wars had insights that would later prove true for vast numbers of other peoples in diaspora. The state of exile in itself forces the necessary questions on the writer. Often, as mentioned at the outset of this chapter, it is the diasporic condition in itself that is the source of inspiration to the artist. Dislocation as muse is spoken of very directly in the stunning interview Paul Auster conducted with Edmond Jabès in 1978, in fact. There Jabès, who was exiled from Egypt because he was Jewish, explains that his books "came into being as a result of this break...as a result of my having to leave this country because I was a Jew" (146). Jabès goes so far as to assert that the Jewish condition—homelessness, dislocation, nomadism, the reliance on books instead of place—is also the writer's condition. He explains it this way:

> I feel a little lost living in Paris, even though I am surrounded by friends and feel comfortable there. It is not my landscape, not my place, my true place. In a sense, I am now living out the historical Jewish condition. The book has become my true place...practically my only place. This idea has become very important to me, to such an extent, in fact, that the condition of being a writer has little by little become almost the same for me as the condition of being a Jew. I feel that every writer in some way experiences the Jewish condition, because every writer, every creator, lives in a kind of exile. (149)

It is a reality to those with the experience of exile that leaving home, creating absence, and dislocation is essential for the writing act to proceed in the first place, and to become meaningful. Eudora Welty, who lived her life in the American South and who did not herself move far from home, nonetheless knew this about writing and the creative process. She has harsh words for writers who will not move out of the familiar, the limits of their experience, when she adjures in "Place in Fiction" that "for the artist to be unwilling to move, mentally or spiritually or physically, out of the familiar is a sign that spiritual timidity or poverty or decay has come upon him; for what is familiar will then have turned into all that is tyrannical" (*Eye* 129). Welty becomes most articulate on the issue of place, movement, belonging, and the writer over the course of her essays. She was herself a very fine photographer as well as writer, and her photographs show her understanding of dislocation and insecurity. She photographed African Americans in their home towns, often in conditions of poverty, wearing the clothing of the bourgeoisie of the South. She knew about conditions of insecurity and asks, "is there a conception more stupefying than that of security?" (132). Perhaps this is what has made the art of African Americans so dynamic, is the underlying suggestion. "No art ever came out of not risking your neck," she claims (132).

Conversely, Welty speaks of the wanderer-writer in the same manner. It is "the stranger within the gates" who can see what regular inhabitants cannot. In Welty's words:

> It may be the stranger within the gates whose eye is smitten by the crucial thing, the essence of life, the moment or act in our long-familiar midst that will forever define it. The inhabitant who has taken his fill of a place and gone away may look back and see it for good, from afar, still there in the mind's eye like a city over the hill. It was in the New Zealand stories, written eleven thousand miles from home and out of homesickness, that Katherine Mansfield came into her own. (130)

Welty also discusses James Joyce, who wrote about Dublin as if he had never left. However, Joyce translated Dublin into "a country of his own" (130).

Joyce's novel *A Portrait of the Artist as a Young Man* is, in fact, a kind of dissertation in itself of the necessity of exile for the artist. If he (the writer) cannot be thrown out, like Lucifer, from the sight of God, then he will throw himself out. Stephen Dedalus, the artist-hero of the novel, exclaims in the end when he has decided to leave home as a prerequisite for becoming a writer, that:

> I will not serve that in which I no longer believe whether it call itself my home, my fatherland or my church: and I will try to express myself in some mode of life or art as freely as I can and as wholly as I can, using for my defense the only arms I allow myself to use— silence, exile, and cunning. (268-69)

About the hero of Joyce's novel, Seamus Deane, Keugh Professor of Irish Studies at the University of Notre Dame, Indiana, writes that the young writer is "an insider who only becomes himself when he becomes an outsider" (x).

The necessity for Stephen to make himself an exile, an outsider, is inscribed in the fact that Ireland as he experiences it is a colonized country and culture. Speaking English is, in itself, a problem of identity, even though English is the writer's language. The reality of a colonized experience of language is described sensitively when the young artist is listening to his dean at school, who is from Britain and speaks the British English, when Stephen says to himself:

> The language in which we are speaking is his before it is mine. How different are the words *home, Christ, ale, master,* on his lips and on mine! I cannot speak or write these words without unrest of spirit. His language, so familiar and so foreign, will always be for me an acquired speech. I have not made or accepted its words. My voice holds them at bay. My soul frets in the shadow of his language. (205)

It is necessary to remove himself from the experience of inauthenticity that is made invisible at home, and go to where dislocations are visible. There, in some other country and in yet another linguistic space, he can do what he needs to do in writing, which is to be himself. As he exclaims: "This race and this country and this life produced me...and I shall express myself as I am" (220). Sometimes going away is the only way of seeing yourself "as you are."

Being essentially yourself means living in congruence with your imagination. When the life of the imagination itself is elevated to the status of memory, history, reality, belonging, as writers so frequently argue, then we have come close to an idea mentioned often by Paul Auster—that the world may actually lie (or exist) in books. Reality is written and imagined before it is seen and shared. For Jewish writers in particular, for whom exile has been a continuous condition, it is

*Is writing going away?*

possible to see the world of books as the homeland itself, or the nation to which one belongs. It is Edmond Jabès who points out, as Auster makes note of, that "in the long interval between exile and the coming of the Messiah, the people of God had become the people of the Book. For Jabès, this meant that the Book had taken on all the weight and importance of a homeland" (109).

Italo Calvino, the Italian writer who has, along with Argentinian Jorge Juis Borges, charted a path in early postmodernism, has also measured the value of the imagination for a writer in aesthetic terms, which amplifies what Annie Dillard claims is a necessity. Calvino argues, in *Six Memos for the Next Millennium*, that one of the most important elements in good writing is a sense of lightness. For him, it is necessary for good writing to remove the weightiness of the reality that surrounds him, and to make that reality light and airy instead. In his poetic way, he thinks of "writing as a metaphor of the powder-fine substance of the world" (26). To achieve that airiness, Calvino claims the writer needs to lighten language itself. He wants "a verbal texture that seems weightless" (16). Since literature is also "a search for knowledge" (26), there is ample cause for him to argue that the life of the imagination, of memory, and the construction of a more refined heterocosm is more durable and more real than "the privation actually suffered" (27). In other words, the life of the imagination becomes more real than phenomenal reality itself.

This notion of the juncture of reality and fiction is also highlighted by Chinua Achebe when he discusses racism in his essay "The Truth of Fiction." Achebe points out that the discourses within which we function in reality are fictions, only we do not acknowledge them as such. He claims that "what distinguishes beneficent fiction from such malignant cousins as racism is that the first never forgets that it is fiction and the other never knows that it is" (148). Achebe believes we should be able to say to ourselves "let us pretend" as we say grace, before we act (151).

One of the barbs diasporic writers often encounter is the accusation of being removed in person from the surroundings of the imaginary work, which presumably makes the writer less knowledgeable. That the writer away from home, in fact, no longer knows what he is talking about. He is no longer an expert. A response to this view might be that the very notion of "expert" is suspect. The idea of the expert has been pushed on the populace in a kind of power struggle, wherein the so-called non-expert is left disempowered. Canadian essayist John Ralston

Saul has talked about the problem of the "expert" at length in his book *The Unconscious Civilization*, his 1995 Massey lectures on the subject of truth and consciousness in modern life. As Saul starkly puts it, "today's power uses as its primary justification for doing wrong the knowledge possessed by its experts" (45).[10]

Chinua Achebe explains the idea of the expert with similar dynamism, but with a different focus, when discussing African writing in his book of essays *Hopes and Impediments*. In his universe, the advent of the expert is turned around, where the European or American is sent into Africa as an expert in something (priests, scholars, scientists, technicians, explorers, journalists), and the locals have to listen. For both writers, what the idea of the expert does, in so many words, is to eliminate dialogue. Bringing in an expert is, to Achebe, an evasion "to replace or simulate dialogue" to the expert's advantage (25). Similarly, writers in exile often find their voice removed and replaced with the monologue (or master discourse) of the home community. In both cases, the idea of knowledge is used to eliminate real dialogue and to disempower the perceived "other." The testimony of the "other" is excluded (26).

Italo Calvino argues that it is the nature of literature, of writing, as it is of all art, to be dislocated. The writer has to be removed from her surroundings in order to write in the first place, he maintains. "Certainly literature would never have existed," he says, "if some human beings had not been strongly inclined to introversion, discontented with the world as it is, inclined to forget themselves for hours and days on end and to fix their gaze on the immobility of silent words" (52).  There is no such thing as accuracy of expression, because everyone sees things differently. The best and only thing a writer can do is be true to her own perception, and that requires introspection. He acknowledges the removal, as it were, of tradition for the modern writer, and maintains that since we have broken with authority, the life of the imagination is more important than ever. This is a time "when literature no longer refers back to an authority or a tradition as its origin or goal," he writes, and so writing "aims at novelty, originality, and invention" (86).

Eudora Welty also discusses this idea of the verbal structure as an independent creation which is not particularly representational or even mimetic, in an essay on the short story, "Looking at Short Stories." Welty spoke of the unfortunate position of the writer in the southern United States who, by virtue of being a white Southerner, is hated by the rest of the nation on account of the civil rights issue, and has to write in spite of that national dislike. Being hated creates hatred in turn, she says, and the Southerner is "trapped" in "venom," which is "a devastating emotion" for a writer (155). One response is to elevate the verbal creation, hoping it will bridge political barriers. Welty writes that "prose is a structure in its every part," and "the imagination is engineered when we write." In fact, "a sentence may be in as perfect control as a church or a bridge" (103).[11] The written text, in her view, stands apart from history and is independent—a structure both sacred and necessary.

Pointing out this juncture, and asserting the necessity of the imagination over tradition, authority, and history (which in any case is problematized by inevitable subjectivity), is essential when we think of the position of the diasporic writer. Whose tradition? Whose remembered authority? The homeland, the land of residence, the mystified and historicized community, the competing master discourses, the clashing cultures, are all at work in the imagination of the writer-in-absentia. The question for such an author is essentially one of identity. As Chinua Achebe points out in his essay "The Writer and His Community," the multicultural milieu and the attendant dislocations that migrations create, forces the question: "Who is my community?" (59). He articulates the problem this way: "If I write novels in a country in which most citizens are illiterate, who then is my community? If I write in English in a country in which English may still be called a foreign language, or in any case is spoken only by a minority, what use is my writing?" (59-60). He is here talking about modern Nigeria, but the question is transferable to any number of countries. He tells the story of a master singer who comes to perform in a large auditorium, only to discover that three-quarters of his audience is deaf. Does he go on with the show for the final one-quarter (36)?

This is the dilemma, I submit, that faces the diasporic writer, for whom Achebe's description of an audience may be quite accurate. My own answer to Achebe's question has always been "yes," but it is not without its discouragements. Even when the writer is living at home, and is not dislocated geographically, there may be dislocations inherent in the home itself that create diasporic conditions anyway. This is commented on by Mario Vargas Llosa in his essay "On Being Nine and First Seeing the Sea." He is explaining how he wanted to be a writer already as a student and wrote poems and stories as a young man. But Peru has had the polarized economy of other South

American countries, which has a sharp division between the very rich and the very poor, with a disproportionately small middle class. Vargas Llosa confesses that "it is quite difficult to think about being a writer if one is born in a country where hardly anyone reads—the poor because they do not know how or lack the means of doing it; and the rich because they do not care to. In that kind of society, to want to be a writer is not choosing a profession but an act of madness" (*Writer's* 64).

There is an argument to be made for the idea that the diasporic writer has, by necessity, a better perspective than more home-grown writers can achieve. Certain basic and, by now, most relevant questions are forced on the writer-in-absentia. When you question your own identity, culture, language, traditions, nationality, community, mores, habits, etc., you are asking the right questions. Migration became a human condition by the end of the twentieth century. Hannah Arendt talks about this condition in relation to the Jewish writers in Europe, who reviewed these problems early. She writes:

> What was decisive was that these men [Jewish intellectuals in pre-war Europe] did not wish to "return" either to the ranks of the Jewish people or to Judaism, and could not desire to do so—not because they believed in "progress" and an automatic disappearance of anti-Semitism or because they were too "assimilated" and too alienated from their Jewish heritage, *but because all traditions and cultures as well as all "belonging" had become equally questionable to them.* (36, my italics)

Not only does the diasporic thinker, artist, writer begin to question "traditions and cultures" and the idea of "belonging," but in fact the whole of Western tradition is open to enquiry. To put it bluntly, posing such basic questions involves the kind of open-mindedness that is necessary for relevance. What Walter Benjamin had to do, in Arendt's words, to discover "that the break in tradition and the loss of authority which occurred in his lifetime were irreparable," is something every writer in diaspora has to find out all over again. As a consequence, he needs "to discover new ways of dealing with the past" (38). The diasporic writer therefore has an edge over the homebound writer. It is every writer's task to "discover new ways of dealing with the past," and to bring into the open that the past is a fiction, but a public fiction. History is a communal memory, but memory just the same, subject to the same flaws, gaps, subjectivities, power struggles, and political fictions that all memory possesses. So fiction itself is its own history, but a history of the emotions, dreams, desires, and nightmares of a community. Fiction is also the subjective truth itself, which is no less true than an agreed-upon version, and possibly more true than any master discourse might be.

# 3 | The Home and the Artist

In a 1998 feature on historic houses, *Architectural Digest* carried an article on the Le Cannet home of French painter Pierre Bonnard.[1] For the last twenty years of his life, Bonnard lived on the Cote d'Azur in a relatively modest house he acquired in 1926. From then on, he painted the interior of that house in every detail. According to his grandnephew Michel Terrace, "there is not a window, a radiator or a cupboard that didn't appear in his paintings" (Solomon, 46-48). He is depicted in this article as not "just a diffident stay-at-home but a visionary of domestic life" (46). There are two curious aspects to the story of Pierre Bonnard and his home. One is that he seems to be among the very few French artists who was not a bohemian. In fact, he "celebrated the bourgeois ideals of French living" in his work (50). The other curious feature is that his life was apparently not like his portrayal of it. While his paintings show warm domesticity, his own home life was anything but serene. On that score, it seems a commonly held opinion that Bonnard was painting in order to "idealize a kind of pleasure he never knew," and that his paintings portray "a desire to will himself into a circle of human warmth" (52). According to this article, "he painted the world he craved" (53).

The idea of art as desire, or that the artist creates what she most desires but cannot, or does not, have, is perhaps a feature in the story of Pierre Bonnard. It is also possible, however, that for him, as for other painters, writers, creators, the home constitutes a necessary nexus of creative energy. That is, the home offers the artist his way of life, and life and art do merge during the creative process. When it comes to writing, for example, it was Virginia Woolf who articulated this in a memorable way when she spoke of the necessity of "a room of one's own." The writer needs a private space, and the home is often it. In her essay "Professions for Women," Woolf explains the writer's needs this way:

*Notes to chapter 3 are on p. 110.*

a novelist's chief desire is to be as unconscious as possible. He has
to induce in himself a state of perpetual lethargy. He wants life to
proceed with the utmost quiet and regularity. He wants to see the
same faces, to read the same books, do the same things day after day,
month after month, while he is writing, so that nothing may break
the illusion in which he is living—so that nothing may disturb or
disquiet the mysterious nosings about, feelings round, darts, dashes,
and sudden discoveries of that very shy and illusive spirit, the imagination. (6)

In other words, predictability, placidity, regularity, tranquility,
become necessary on the outside so the imagination can have free play
on the inside. As Bessie Head confesses in her preface to "Witchcraft,"
republished in her book of essays *A Woman Alone*, "I like a repetition
of everyday events—the weather, the sunrise, or going to the same spot
every day" (27).[2] And later she adds: "Here, in the steadiness and peace
of my own world, I could dream dreams a little ahead of the somewhat
vicious clamour of revolution and the horrible stench of evil social systems" (28). For this, the writer's home becomes not only central, but a
sanctuary. In another essay, Head confesses that "I need a quiet back-
water and a sense of living as though I am barely alive on the earth, tread-
ing a small, careful pathway through life" (77). The remarkable thing
about these observations is that the most bourgeois and staid artist,
Bonnard in France, has the same needs as the most challenged, mixed-
race, woman writer living as a refugee, Head in Botswana. The great
diversity in their backgrounds does not change the fact that, as Virginia
Woolf points out, a writer needs peace, quiet, and predictable routine
around her.

The same idea is voiced by Wallace Stegner in a series of interviews
he did for Dartmouth College on the subject of creative writing in the
universities. Stegner, who taught writing for over forty years, came to
the conclusion that: "I know no way to become convinced, and stay convinced, of the reality and worthiness of a novel but to go out every
morning to the place where writing is done, and put your seat on the
seat of the chair, as Sinclair Lewis advised, and keep it there" (40). In
general, he adds that every writer "will benefit from a good, deep, well-
worn, and familiar rut" (41). Such ruts and routines are best found in
life at home. It is hard to see how a whole writing life can be carved out
of a series of "retreats" away from home.

The "well-worn rut" that a writer has at home, and the peace and
quiet she needs so her imagination is not disturbed, as Woolf adjures,

is exemplified by Marguerite Duras in her essay "Writing." Duras writes about her house Neauphle, which she bought with her writer's earnings ten years prior to writing her essay. She tells of how she grew into her house and how her writing, how certain of her books, have sprung from this home organically. She describes it like this:

> One does not find solitude, one creates it. Solitude is created alone. I have created it. Because I decided that *here* was where I should be alone, that I would be alone to write books. It happened this way. I was alone in this house. I shut myself in—of course, I was afraid. And then I began to love it. This house became the house of writing. My books come from this house. From this light as well, and from the garden. (4)

The freedom of working at home is very real to Duras on the political as well as the psychological level. The writer at home is the opposite of "the hell and injustice of the working world" (30). The home offers the creative person "deliverance." She points out that "We can write at any hour of the day. We are not sanctioned by orders, schedules, bosses, weapons, fines, insults, cops, bosses, and bosses" (31). So even though the solitude and aloneness a writer feels in the house can be literally maddening, Duras is convinced of the complete necessity of it. The freedom found in working at home is for her unparalleled.

The notion that it is possible to achieve the solitude and tranquility necessary for creative work, such as writing, in the home is carried further by the tradition of the study itself—a room in the house where this writing is done. In a 1998 book on the history of the study by Dora Thornton, *The Scholar in His Study: Ownership and Experience in Renaissance Italy*, the idea of the study is traced to its origins in the patriarchal home of sixteenth-century Europe. The source for information about the Renaissance study comes from inventories made by the office of wards of Florence and Venice. Thornton also resorted to account books and memoranda, which show that it was not necessary to be wealthy in order to have a study. The inventories she looked at informed her of how studies were furnished. The study had various names, according to its position in the house and the intimacy it provided. The Florentine house had anything from the more public *sala* on the first floor, and the more private *camera principale* (bed-chamber), within which could be found the very private *camerino*, or English "closet" and the French *cabinet*. These private rooms approximate the study, or the *studio* or *studiolo*.

The principal aim of the *studiolo* is articulated by Montaigne, and quoted by James Fenton in a review of Thornton's book in *The New York Review of Books*. Montaigne describes the function of the study this way:

> We should set aside a room, just for ourselves, at the back of the shop, keeping it entirely free and establishing there our true liberty, our principle [sic] solitude and asylum. Within it our normal conversation should be of ourselves, with ourselves, so privy that no commerce or communication with the outside world should find a place there; there we should talk and laugh as though we had no wife or children, no possessions, no followers, no menservants, so that when the occasion arises that we must lose them it should not be a new experience to do without them. We have a soul able to turn in on herself; she can keep herself company; she has the wherewithal to attack, to defend, to receive and to give.[3]

The idea of a study sounds very patriarchal, and is meant to allow the patriarch to check out of the domestic scene without leaving home. But the need for a private space like a study is universal and human. Solitude for creative purposes is not necessarily found in a "room," if rooms are not available. But this discussion is confined to "houses" as we know them in modernity. In other cultures, privacy may be found in many ways, but I suggest the principle is universal. It is well known, for example, that Sarah Roosevelt, FDR's mother, who inherited and ran the family estate in Hyde Park after her husband's death, retreated into her private "snuggery" to do the household accounts. There is also the tradition of the more elaborate "counting house," which is a separate study built off the main house, where the patriarch can go and, ostensibly, do his accounts, but which was often used as a private retreat for other purposes as well. In an interview with Maya Angelou for *Home and Garden TV*, Angelou says very directly that everyone should have a place that is "inviolate," a private space to retreat to, where creativity can occur. To Angelou, that is a place where you go and meet God, and for that reason it has to be inviolate—safe from any husband, employer, child, or friend.

The private room, the study, the snuggery, has been imagined and acted out as a place where one may be private, have private conversations, meet God, pray, dream, and consequently be creative. The relationship between the home and the ability to dream is brought up again by author and journalist Kennedy Fraser in a guest essay for the May

1999 issue of *Architectural Digest*. Fraser describes how, even though she lives in New York, she has bought a home in Whitby, England, a seaside town which is a lot like a place she has dreamed of in the past. Her roots are English, and her most primary dreams and memories are, she says, English. She describes her relationship to the house she has bought this way:

> For years and years I had a recurrent dream: I was back in my native England, in some house by the sea; and I was with my mother. I would climb the stairs in a tall Victorian house to stand at the threshold of a big room—a room with a view, where I could write the things I dreamed of writing. (44)

Dreaming, writing, and desiring come together in the actual house she has purchased and renovated. For Fraser, these three appear to be intricately connected. But she is not alone in thinking so. The same sentiment is voiced by Leslie Marmon Silko in a brief essay called "Breaking Down the Boundaries: 'Earth, Air, Water, Mind'," published in a collection of essays on the story, called *The Tales We Tell*.[4] Silko claims that "in order to be a writer you cannot jar the body or move it around. The closer you can be to the dream state, to waking up, the better, and so nightgowns are good. Actually no clothes at all are, but I try loose-fitting clothes" (91). For both writers, Kennedy Fraser who is English and Leslie Marmon Silko who is Native American, life at home and the writing act are inescapably, intricately linked.

The idea that the home itself is the most important place for a writer is contradicted in the persistence of the popular myth of the café society that has grown around bohemianism and art. We think of writers spending huge amounts of time in cafés, and the image has caught the public imagination. In fact, many writers do write whole books in cafés, and many writers claim to spend their writing time in public places. So while this is not necessarily a myth, it might benefit from being put into context. An essay by Hungarian-Canadian writer George Jonas, which appeared in the 10 June 2000 issue of *Saturday Night*, follows up on this mythology of writers and cafés. Jonas claims to have no real "restaurant" to hang out in in Canada, like they did in continental Europe, and he laments the fact. He explains how everyone where he comes from used restaurants as social gathering places and creative watering holes:

> One did not need to be particularly bohemian to spend much time in restaurants in my part of the world. In post-war Europe, homes and offices were often crowded, dilapidated, and depressing. Clubs,

popular in Britain, were uncommon on the continent. Many people worked and socialized in restaurants.

Cafés were not only for writers and artists. Even hog merchants, civil servants, and travelling salesmen used a favourite eatery for their headquarters. (64)

So the "restaurant" acquired as many formulations as the home "study," and could be anything from a bistro to a brasserie, pub, trattoria, tavern, boîte, canteen, greasy spoon, beanery, hash slinger, or low boozer. But the important note Jonas strikes is to remind us that café life for artists and others became popular between the wars because the economy of Europe was bad, people were poor, families were large, housing was, as he says, "crowded, dilapidated, and depressing." We need only think of a novel like Beryl Bainbridge's *A Quiet Life* to be reminded of the need people on the European continent and Britain had for a place away from home that was warm and social. The English wartime home in Bainbridge's novel is so cold that the family must huddle in a tiny kitchen where there is not enough room for a chair for everyone. The living room is closed off and family members wear mittens and scarves inside. The mother of the family ends up going out in the evenings to the local railway station, which is warm and bright, where she can read her books. Ernest Hemingway also describes, in *A Moveable Feast*, how his flat in Paris is so cold that he goes out in the morning to write in a restaurant, where it is warm. However, before the industrial revolution, before the Depression, and after the Second World War, the home could again resume its function as the sustaining site for the creative and spiritual life. Perhaps Jonas's inability to find one "restaurant" or "bistro" to hang out in in Toronto attests to the fact that homes in modern North America are generally comfortable and roomy enough to take back the function they had in the nineteenth century.

There is, however, a force acting on modern life which is in opposition to the enjoyment of home and neighborhood as a sacred space for creation or for meditation. Bill Kauffmann, in an essay called "Passport to Main Street," names that force the insurgence of "placism." The globalization of corporate culture, he maintains, has made it necessary and desirable to move away from home to where the jobs are. Anyone who stays where he is born is suspect in this new society. Kauffmann writes that the "placists" and their mobile institutions are welcome to their world. But they will not let the rest of us be. For almost sixty years, the placeless have waged war on the rooted, stealing their children, devastating their neighborhoods, wiping out local peculiarities and idiosyncrasies. The onslaught has included bussing, consolidation of schools, the interstate highway system, subsidizing of colleges and universities, public housing construction that displaces the urban poor and shatters working-class neighbourhoods. (54-55)

Kaufmann himself lives and writes in New York where he comes from, and draws his inspiration from his own neighborhood. This "rootedness" is conducive, he claims, not just to creativity, but to a holding together of the universe which is necessary for mind and soul.

When discussing matters of the "soul," a concept brought back recently into general usage with a vengeance, Thomas Moore claims in his book *Care of the Soul* that it is this sense of the everyday, the particular, the ordinary, which contains the memories of our lives, our childhoods, and our ancestors, which the "soul" needs in order to be "alive." As with Pierre Bonnard, who drew inspiration from the most ordinary objects in his home, we all need that rooted ordinariness to be inspired. Moore cites Lynda Sexson's book *Ordinarily Sacred,* to say that we need to have a physical location for what is sacred to us. Perhaps a box that holds special letters, or an album that holds meaningful photographs, would be the smallest manifestation of what in a larger sense is the home itself. Moore places high value on what he calls this kind of "vernacular spirituality" that would permit us to live out our spiritual existence in the ordinary, domestic objects and events of everyday life (215). He also reminds us that creativity and religion are close cousins, and religion is, in essence, an "art of memory" (214). It is the home, and beyond it the neighborhood and the region, that contains those memories that are the basic building blocks of "soul."

The home, for Thomas Moore, is the ultimate site for creativity. He warns that we need to be "mindful of the importance of beauty in our homes" (271) because too great an emphasis on function will deplete us of our aesthetic selves. The home is the most important crossroads of the vernacular and the universal for a person. "Many traditions," he notes, "acknowledge the archetypal nature of a house with some kind of cosmic ornament—a sun and moon, a band of stars, a dome that obviously reflects the canopy of the sky" (271). He suggests, for that reason, that "we should all have images in our houses that remind us of our relationship to the cosmos" and cites Marsilio

Ficino for this idea (271-72).[5] According to Moore, Ficino suggested that we should have "a model of the universe or an astrological painting" in our homes to remind us of the connection with the cosmos, because "a real home is always at once a particular place and the entire world" (272). As so many artists and writers attest, the home is both a place that is desired, and a place to escape from through the imagination. As well, these artists have shown that for them, the home is the dream made reality, and the site for all possible accomplishments.

# 4 | Transcultural Appropriation
## Problems and Perspectives

Literary appropriation, wherein a writer uses material and a language that does not derive from his own background or culture, is an issue with more than one side to it. Appropriation in language and literature carries with it, as Ashcroft, Griffiths, and Tiffin point out in their early text on postcolonial literatures, *The Empire Writes Back*, "the curious tension of cultural 'revelation' and cultural 'silence'" (59). We speak of appropriation by the centre of the margins, in postcolonial studies. By this we mean that writers in the mainstream, colonizing, imperial societies, whose language is dominant and who are working from a centre of power, will sometimes use the cultural material of non-mainstream, colonized societies, and render their stories in the dominant language and sell them in the imperial marketplace. Marginalized cultures may see this use of their private material as an act of theft, leaving them even more silenced and disempowered. There is therefore an ethical problem with the appropriation of the margins by the centre.

On the other hand, literary appropriation by the margins of the centre carries another dimension, which is more positive and can be a political tool as well as a literary act. A writer in a marginalized culture may tell his own stories, or stories from his own "outsider" culture, but tell them in the dominant language. Using a language not his own will alter both the language and the stories told, but the responsibility and the power rest with the writer in the margins. What happens is the dominant language is changed by the way it is used by its colonized people. What follows is an outline of the notion of literary appropriation from both angles. This kind of two-way street regarding the issue of appropriation for writers simplifies what happens in literature, which is beyond the ability of critics to outline. In the frequently quoted words of Nadine Gordimer, "great art must strive to transcend such boundaries." The interactions between people at all levels are not exactly controllable,

*Notes to chapter 4 are on p. 110.*

*All boundaries*

43

and one has the feeling that those with strong opinions on the rights or wrongs of appropriation in writing are trying to exert control over something perhaps best left ambiguous. As Gordimer says: "Although the law has kept us, in some ways very successfully apart, there's an enormous area of life where…on farms and in town, we have been rubbing up against each other in a vast area where our consciousness is intermingled" (14-15).

## Appropriation of the Margins by the Centre

In his interview with Edmond Jabès, Paul Auster asks why Jabès wrote *The Book of Questions*. Jabès answers by referring to a comment made by Maurice Blanchot, to the effect that "when two people talk, one of them must always remain silent" (152). Jabès explains how the listener gets more and more silenced the longer the talker talks, until all questions disappear. This is a notion Christa Wolf has spoken of as well, in a political context. At the heart of the problem of appropriation in writing, it is the relationship between speaker and listener, writer and reader, which is central. The person who tells a story becomes the person who owns it, regardless of accuracy, veracity, or appropriateness. The question of the writer's responsibility in relation to the ownership of stories is also a question of ethics.

*[margin note: Politicians + Bores!]*

Lee Maracle, who is outspoken on the issue of cultural appropriation from the Native Canadian perspective, tackled this issue in 1989 with an essay titled "Native Myths: Trickster Alive and Crowing," which continues to be republished.[1] Maracle is adamant that the question of appropriation of voice involves more than ethics. There is a very deep problem with writers using and taking over the material of other cultures and other voices, she argues. In her words, "the truth is that creeping around libraries full of nonsensical anthropocentric drivel, imbuing these findings with falsehood in the name of imagination, then peddling the nonsense as 'Indian Mythology' is literary dishonesty" (314). She goes so far as to consider appropriation of voice a "crime," something akin to a "war crime" committed in times of "peace." She argues that "the laws against plagiarism were born to protect the intellectual integrity of the literary community. To cry 'censorship' when caught trafficking in such truck is at best cowardly" (314). Lee Maracle is not alone in her use of strong language to describe the issue from the perspective of the indigenous person. In a useful anthology on appropriation titled *Borrowed Power: Essays on Cultural Appropriation*, Bruce Ziff and Pratima V. Rao, editors of this volume, have collected a large variety of observations from writers and scholars, as well as a good bibliography for further reading. Contributors to this collection argue, as part of the larger picture, that "the term 'appropriation' hardly seems adequate in comparison to the descriptive accuracy of others, including brutal expropriation and outright theft" (Cuthbert 257).

When fellow writer Timothy Findley critiqued Maracle by calling her objections "fascist," she countered that not only is the theft of Native cultural material by non-Native writers unethical and basically criminal, but such theft constitutes a form of new imperialism which is both economic and racist. Writers who are not mindful of the real meaning of the idea of "appropriation" are simply aiding in the process of cultural "genocide." Maracle insists that "our stories had original authors; we are not dead. Someone told these stories to someone else who reaped copyright, royalties, credit and the dubious privilege of bastardizing them. We have lost both revenue and dignity in the process" (314). To watch your own cultural material being bandied about by people not in your community may seem like a way of being "othered" inside your own country. It is not surprising that she would also identify the economic drain that such a loss of vitality for Native writers represents. The whole idea of appropriation, therefore, strikes her as simply racist. She argues that "to continue appropriating our stories and misusing them in the name of 'freedom of imagination' is just so much racism" (314).

Timothy Findley, however, who comes up as one of Maracle's targets in her attempt to justify her position against appropriation, has made some distinctions of his own. In a lecture on writing at Humber College of the Arts (broadcast on the Knowledge Network in a series on "The Writing Life"). Findley talks about his novel *Famous Last Words*, and how he had taken material from Ezra Pound and used it in his fiction. In explaining this process for a fiction writer, Findley maintains a distinction between plagiarism and stealing. Plagiarism, he asserts, is a sin, but stealing is fine. Theft is all right provided the victim's name is "shouted" from the rooftops and proper acknowledgement is made. Plagiarism, on the other hand, is a condition wherein a writer is using material not her own, and does not acknowledge the source anywhere. That kind of usage is, Findley agrees, unjustifiable. The major task for the writer, he asserts, is to be able to "imagine more."

To "imagine more" is also the imaginative writer's task, and this means deconstructing barriers of all kinds in the way we think. There are many successful books that break the glass wall of gender and race.

Titles like *Anna Karenina, Memoirs of a Geisha,* and *The Temptations of Big Bear,* instantly spring to mind. But to follow up on the argument made by Lee Maracle: when such work is very good and very successful, that does not eliminate the problem or lessen the pain of what she is naming. On the contrary, the successful execution of an "appropriative" work makes the problems involved—ethical, psychological, economic, and social—even worse. The experience of "racism" that Maracle claims is invoked in being "appropriated" is just as bad when the one who has "used" you is being praised, lauded, or admired as it is when she is being criticized or brutalized. For example, over a year after Arthur Golden's novel *Memoirs of a Geisha* appeared, which is narrated from the point of view of a Japanese geisha who tells her secrets to us, one of Golden's "informants" sued him for appropriating her. The Japanese woman whom he interviewed for his material claimed that Golden had violated a verbal agreement and told too much to the world, leaving her exposed and therefore damaging her.

The notion of racism requires serious philosophical and psychosocial consideration, and it is probably true that many of us are glib about the concept and use the word before its implications are fully understood. One of the features of racism, and also of "appropriation" when the appropriative act is successful, is, for example, described by Bharati Mukherjee.[2] Mukherjee has written, in "An Invisible Woman," that her experience of being an Indian woman in white Canada made life paradoxical for her in certain ways. She explains that "the oldest paradox of prejudice is that it renders its victims simultaneously invisible and overexposed" (325). To live in a hollowed-out shell like that is bound to be seriously debilitating. Says Mukherjee: "I cannot describe the agony and the betrayal one feels" (328). She talks about acquiring an inner "double-vision when self-perception is so utterly at odds with social standing," and that being in the paradox of invisible overexposure makes us "split from our most confident self-assumptions" (328). It is not hard to imagine how just that feeling of being in a "hollowed shell," at once invisible and overexposed, is precisely what happens to people whose stories are appropriated and told by others.

Bessie Head puts this psychological reality in her own way in a very brief essay from 1963, "An Unspeakable Crime," when speaking of racism and the "coloured man" in South Africa who becomes, under Apartheid, "a timid God-fearing law abiding citizen of his own particular hell" (*Woman* 8). Or even more pointedly, since the suspicion of being ignored and erased carries with it the feeling that one is not wanted, as Head describes in another brief essay, "Letter from South Africa": "you could just cry to be delivered from this unceasing torment of hate, hate, hate" (14). In the face of serious prejudice or, as seems to be the case with appropriation, a real sense of *erasure*, it seems absolutely necessary to voice what these writers are voicing. Saying nothing is not an option. Bessie Head describes the experience of being a target of racism and thereby being made "hollow" so that you see yourself with others' eyes and find it just as hard as outsiders do to somehow "know yourself." She explains that "we did not know who or what we were, apart from objects of abuse and exploitation" (66). It could be argued in connection with this experience that appropriation of stories simply adds to the problems those appropriated have of beginning to see themselves as "objects" without a voice. The relationship between the experience of being "appropriated" in literature and racism is not to be underestimated. My argument here is that, at the very least, the issue of appropriation needs to be handled with care and concern and a full understanding of what it entails.

While the issue of appropriation for the "victim," involving as it does a kind of personally felt "robbery," invasion of privacy, infiltration, unethical behaviour, imperialism, cultural/imagerial "genocide," and just plain racism, the issues are just as complex for the writer on the other side of the issue. The one who appropriates material from other cultures or other individuals is, in many ways, simply acting out the writer's functions. To explain the "benefits," or even the necessity, of being free to take material from wherever one wishes and use it in any way necessary, is to some a "sacred trust" of the writer. Paul Auster talks about this in the context of the French poet Segalen, for example, in his essay "Twentieth-Century French Poetry."[3] The point about Segalen is that he "wrote behind the mask of another culture" because he had to (215). That is, his poems were "poems written by a French poet *as if he were Chinese*" (216). The poet had to efface himself behind the "mask" of another culture in order to be able to cover a larger imaginary territory. Auster explains that "by freeing himself from the limitations of his own culture, by circumventing his own historical moment, Segalen was able to explore a much wider territory—to discover, in some sense, that part of himself that was a poet" (216). Many writers have felt a need to truly be away from their own milieu because being locked in your own environment can seem limiting and can work against the creative impulse. Trying to limit the imaginary universe of another is, to many writers, just as much a crime as it is for others to be appropriated.

A good example of someone writing behind the "mask" of another culture and in that way exploring a much wider territory is Arthur Golden's *Memoirs of a Geisha*.[4] Golden, an American white man, writes from the point of view of a Japanese woman. In an interview with the Knowledge Network, Golden was asked about appropriation, and how he got the nerve to write what he did. He claimed that the old adage "write what you know" was bad advice, and that in his view that would be limiting. However, he added, you should definitely "know what you write." Golden is joined in this, argumentatively, by another contemporary example of similar dimensions. Canadian poet Robert Bringhurst has, as he says, spent fifteen years of his life learning the Haida language and writing up the oral literature of the Haida, as told to Swanton in 1900 and 1901.[5] Bringhurst argues that you cannot tell a writer what to work on, and you cannot expect him to collaborate. "A writer has to think for himself," Bringhurst said to an audience in BC in August 2000, when asked about this problem.

Some writers will argue, in fact, that there is no difference at heart between people of different cultures. All it takes is clarity and honesty (and hard work) to find the common thread and humanity that unites us all. For example, American author Susan Richards Shreve wrote an essay for the *New York Times* series "Writers on Writing," wherein she confesses to having written a novel from the point of view of a black woman.[6] Since she herself is white, when her "long-time editor" read the manuscript, he turned the book down because it was too risky in his view to publish a novel appropriated like that. So for Shreve, the issue of appropriation was about being published in the first place, let alone being criticized for what you have written. She took on a pseudonym and sent the book to another publisher, who, she claims, assumed "initially that she had read an autobiographical novel by a young African-American woman." This rather risky step, she admits, afforded her the experience of the "deep pleasure of anonymity." She explains that the pleasure of not being identified as the author, and hiding behind the mask of anonymity, reminded her of the pleasure of storytelling around the dinner table in her childhood, when she could stop being who she really was for a moment, and be just a pure storyteller. Nadine Gordimer describes this sort of role even more strongly by maintaining:

> How does a writer write from the perspective of a child? How does a writer change sex? How could the famous soliloquy of Molly Bloom have been written by James Joyce? Anybody can write about anything—if they're good enough. Defining authenticity on some

exclusionary basis or other won't change a thing. There's no formula for how you acquire authenticity. (qtd in Johnson n.p.)

The counsel that you should do your own work and know what you write is becoming a kind of mantra for people who agree with Golden and Bringhurst and who are nearly religious about the idea of research, as Timothy Findley insisted in his lecture on writing to the Humber School of Writing. But since the act of appropriation has two sides to it, and the one being "appropriated" experiences real suffering, it would be more than reasonable to suggest that the appropriative writer should go further than simply "know" what she is writing about. She should also respect the problem and acknowledge the potential, and possibly the reality, that some form of abuse is being inflicted—somewhere.

## APPROPRIATION BY THE MARGINS OF THE CENTRE

When we talk about appropriation in relation to writing, this outlined concept that stories and imagination and cultural material can be stolen and used, peddled, owned by others, is not the whole problem of appropriation. In postcolonial studies, appropriation is seen to go the other way as well. That is, when a marginalized writer uses the language and the material of the colonizer, or uses the imperial language and changes it to suit his needs, that writer on the margins is appropriating the material of the centre for his own use. This is considered necessary. The imperial language needs to be decolonized, and by using it abrogatively, the writer may perform a valuable function. In other words, when the centre appropriates from the margins, the existing power structure does not allow for the margin's defence. First, the appropriations have to go from the centre to the margins; writers on the margins need to be able to appropriate from the imperial culture first. Ziff and Rao, in their anthology, include the observation that when it comes to this kind of "appropriation in reverse," we are not so much dealing with appropriation as we are with "the assimilation of culture." As they further argue, the whole cross-directional movement of appropriation does not just go two ways, but is more complex and multidirectional than the original centre-and-margins debate makes it appear. However, for the writer's purposes, that original binary can be useful.

In their book *The Empire Writes Back: Theory and Practice in Post-Colonial Literatures*, Ashcroft, Griffiths, and Tiffin explain what they mean by appropriation. They note that postcolonial writing needs to "define itself by seizing the language of the centre and re-placing it in a discourse fully adapted to the colonized place" (38). What the colonized writer needs to do is "abrogate" the language of the centre, which "involves a rejection of the metropolitan power over the means of communication" (38). After abrogating that language, the writer must appropriate it, which is "the appropriation and reconstitution of the language of the centre, the process of capturing and remoulding the language to new usages," and thus "separate" the colonial language "from the site of colonial privilege" (38). They are talking about a refusal to play the game of the centre; abrogation is a "refusal of the categories of the imperial culture, its aesthetic, its illusory standard of [what is] normative" (38). This is, simply put, a bit like refusing to play the game on the other's terms, in which case, there is no game. On the other hand, appropriation is "the process by which the language is taken and made to 'bear the burden' of one's own cultural experience, or, as Raja Rao puts it, to 'convey in a language that is not one's own the spirit that is one's own.'" (38-39). Or to use the same analogy of a game, by taking the old pieces and creating new rules with them, for one's own use, to serve one's own ends.

When a writer in the margins, or the colonized writer, uses the colonizer's language, several developments occur that are interesting from the creative point of view. One development is that the writer begins to have two faces. Ashcroft and others explain it this way: the cultural location of such a writer "'creates' two audiences and faces two directions, wishing to reconstitute experience through an act of writing which uses the tools of one culture or society and yet seeks to remain faithful to the experience of another" (60-61). Having such a double focus may contain certain self-colonizing elements, which would be interesting to probe.[7] Another development for the "two-faced" writer is that the author becomes an interpreter of his own culture. He becomes an "informant" of sorts, an ethnographer of his own. As such, the writer who appropriates an imperial language to convey a non-imperial experience, is his own first reader. Ashcroft and colleagues describe this phenomenon in the following way:

> The post-colonial writer, whose gaze is turned in two directions, stands already in that position which will come to be occupied by an interpretation, for he/she is not the object of an interpretation, but the first interpreter. Editorial intrusions, such as the footnote, the glossary, and the explanatory preface, where these are made by the author, are a good example of this. Situated outside the

text, they represent a reading rather than a writing, primordial sorties into that interpretive territory in which the Other (as reader) stands. (61)

It should be noted here that postcolonial studies, in the context in which it is treated in the book *The Empire Writes Back,* is focused on imperial centres and colonized margins. However, the problems involved, which are nicely delineated in this book, need not be seen in terms of such binaries. We can think of a novel such as Ha Jin's *Waiting* as an example of "facing in two directions" and "writer as interpreter" and "writer as cultural reader," without posing the problem in terms of power and colonization.[8] China, the setting of Ha Jin's novel, is not a colonized country, and English is not the imperial language here. But there is nonetheless a double facing and interpretation of post-revolutionary China going on here, where Ha Jin, as an American writer of Chinese descent, poses himself as an interpreter of his own background to readers who are unfamiliar with it. We find in his case, as we have found with Amy Tan's *The Joy Luck Club* and Maxine Hong Kingston's *The Warrior Woman,* that some tension exists between Chinese readers and American-Chinese readers, regarding the accuracy of the writer's cultural interpretations. Therefore it is better to speak of a third environment that springs up in such discourses, rather than trying to keep the idea of pure binaries in place. We could, for example, see many cultures feeding off each other and acting simultaneously, with writers and readers being caught between them in various ways, making the issue of appropriation—and who has a right to speak for whom and tell whose stories—very murky indeed. That murkiness is exemplified lightly in a brief study by Ian Almond which appeared in *Orbis Litterarum* in 2002. Almond compares stories by Rudyard Kipling and Raja Rao and shows how they both appropriated in different directions, but for the same purpose (which was to show the superiority of their own cultures and nations; England and India). This kind of project, Almond points out, has only one end result, which is to "expose" the "semantic vacuities within the nationalist project" (285). Claims of superiority, and of "ownership" of certain cultural features, will, he says, lead to the realization that there is nothing there. What arises from the perception of cultural vacuity is "a moment of delayed panic" (286). When one surveys the controversy surrounding appropriation in writing, it is precisely such a note of panic that can be detected on both sides.

The disintegration that occurs in the writer who makes himself so multifaceted that he speaks between several cultures and languages is an invitation to postmodernism. Two modern novels that show interesting examples of dislocation that is both linguistic and cultural, and which show the writer in the act of interpreting cultures in more than one direction, are Kazuo Ishiguro's *When We Were Orphans* and Chang-rae Lee's *A Gesture Life*. Kazuo Ishiguro is from Japan, lives in Britain, and writes in English.[9] In *When We Were Orphans*, he writes of an Englishman who grew up in China and is interpreting through his multivalent lens the culture of the International Settlement in pre-revolutionary Shanghai. In the latter instance, Chang-rae Lee is an American of Korean descent, who writes in *A Gesture Life* about a Japanese-Korean immigrant to the United States, and is interpreting Japanese displacement through his own lens.[10] In *A Gesture Life*, displacement goes in several directions at once, because the protagonist, Kurohati, is an ethnic Korean who grows up in Japan and later immigrates to the USA, where he is known strictly as Japanese-American, all other nuances erased. Here there are appropriations going at least three ways, and these novels show the intricacies that occur in the issues of appropriation. Both authors are, in fact, appropriating cultures not their own, and rendering their "kidnappings" in yet another, a third, culture.

What both these authors are doing, and what happens when an author "interprets" his own culture to another, more central one, is an exploration of dislocation. Ashcroft and others talk about this type of postcolonial literature as being "'about' a void, a psychological abyss between cultures. Ethnographic detail serves not as local colour [which might be seen as forms of self-exoticization], but as the central feature of a structuring" (63). We have therefore moved out of the area of regionalism and local colouring, to something more central to the creative act—which is structure itself. (In fact, discussions involving the language of "ethnicity" and "regionalism" are less than useful here.) We find discordances, which under former circumstances might be seen as creative failures, because they seem to lack the "authenticity" we wish for. In other words, our reading for "authenticity" may be mistaken to begin with, because we cannot see the cultural nuance that is being articulated—we do not recognize it as real yet. Aschcroft et al. warn that we have, in such a case, misread. They note, quoting Canadian poet Dennis Lee, that "the exploration of this gap, its acceptance, and its installation as the legitimate subject-matter of the postcolonial, rather than a sign of failure and inauthenticity, is the crucial act of appropriation" (63).[11]

What these writers have done, in the words of Ashcroft et al., is "seize the language [English], re-place it in a specific cultural location, and yet maintain the integrity of that Otherness, which historically has been employed to keep the post-colonial at the margins of power, of 'authenticity', and even of reality itself" (77). Here an essay by Ingrid Johnston about teaching multicultural literature in the Canadian classroom may be illuminating. She describes her struggles with the issue of authenticity, agency, and literary standards, and opens the problem up to deeper questions of identity, culture, subjectivity and voice. Our whole notion of identity, for example, is part of our Eurocentric baggage. In reality, and she quotes Trinh T. Minh-ha on this, "we need to acknowledge the ambivalence and shifting nature of identity and difference."

## CONCLUSIONS

When we view the problems of appropriation, both from the margins and from the centres, we have a panorama of theoretical concerns that branch into issues of creative writing, of postmodernism, of postcolonialism, cultural studies, and linguistic-semiotic studies—among others. There is a bigger issue involved for the English-language reader (the reader and theorist immersed in the texts of other cultures which are rendered into his own language, and seen from the vantage point of where he is—which is either North America or Britain). The larger issue is not whether it is "right" or "wrong" for writers like Arthur Golden to reinterpret "other" cultures and remake them in their image; or whether it is "accurate" for the transplanted writer to reinterpret her own, former, culture and recast it in our image; or whether the expatriate writer living in the English-language setting is able to authentically carry on this work without getting entangled in the mesh of dislocations that are bound to present themselves. The bigger issue is, instead, both for the scholar and theorist, as Ashcroft, Griffiths, and Tiffin say at the end of their treatment on appropriation, that we are looking at "specific features of texts which constantly address themselves to the task of dismantling those assumptions that have historically constituted 'English literature'" (77). We are, in other words, constantly revising our notions of what our "national" literatures are made of, and where, if anywhere, the boundaries of culture (which we have yet to adequately define as a concept in itself) actually lie.

# 5 | Theory and Fiction
## The Mixed Bag of Postmodern Writing

In the 15 March 1998 issue of the *New York Times Book Review*, Laura Miller, an editor at *Salon*, wrote a rebuttal to a debate she says had been going on for five or six years, about the durability of the novel in relation to a new mutation of the genre called *hyperfiction*. In hyperfiction, a story is told as if it were also literary criticism, and reader participation is involved. No chronology or structure is necessary in hyperfiction, and readers will finally be "liberated" from "linear narrative and the author" (43). These assertions, Miller argues, are claptrap. The novel in its traditional form is not now and never will be dead. "What the laboratory of hyperfiction demonstrates," writes Miller, "is how alienated academic literary criticism is from actual readers and their desires." She further says that the academic reader is "the creature of a world where books are assigned, not chosen. To the academic, a book is often a stony monument from which the relatively insignificant scholar must wring some drop of fresh commentary" (43).[1] Here the author of that week's "Bookend" essay is voicing what is commonly heard in the debate between the populace and the ivory tower "elite," or between the academic and the so-called real reader. The enemy, in what could be seen as a backlash movement against poststructuralism, is literary theory.

One of the understandable arguments in the apparent backlash to post-structuralist writing, which also goes for postmodern "classical" music, is the sense of elitism and exclusion these new modes of art convey. The idea that you have to be an expert in the area before you can enjoy it is unpalatable to many. The sense of exclusion is not only based in ideas but also in language. The populist protest is against what is pejoratively called "jargon," but which is simply the vocabulary of the field for academics. In his strangely hybrid book *The Unconscious Civilization* (hybrid in that it seems to draw on extensive readings in fairly "elitist" subjects in philosophy and ancient science, while proclaiming a populist view), John Ralston Saul says that "obscure language could be reduced to the following formula: obscurity suggests complexity which suggests importance" (49).[2] Further, the apparent anger there is towards high theory (for feelings seem to run high) Saul would explain by suggesting that there is "a sense in the citizenry that they have been abandoned by their thinkers; a sense of being betrayed by an intelligentsia which does not take the humanist experience seriously" (179).

The same argument in classical music was once voiced by Andrew Lloyd Webber, who is quoted in the *New York Times* as having said that the audience for classical music has shrunk because "for forty years of madness...classical music turned its back on audiences" (Griffiths 37). But the author of this article, Paul Griffiths, goes on to defend "new" music, which lacks harmony and melody and structure when compared with the masters of two, three, four hundred years ago, and explains that performing music, like writing books, is about certain vital challenges: "how you present yourself in public, how you argue a case, how you interpret a document, what evidence you accept and what you question, where you draw the limit between what you are told and what you want." Griffiths also reminds us that music, art, is about "the values of asserting the importance of things...that have no physical existence or monetary worth" (37).

Here I wish to raise a defence for the use of literary theory in the practice of fiction. Or, to explain why one might wish to both write and read post-modernist texts. So-called poststructuralist novels have a tendency to overstep their generic limits and start philosophizing outside the stories they are supposed to tell. In a discussion for students of writing where he outlines the properties of a work of fiction, John Gardner claims in *The Art of Fiction* that a story is like a dream, and the dream cannot be interrupted by moments of awkwardness or misplaced language or insertions of the wrong tone. The dream has to proceed in an unbroken manner till the end. The downside of the hypnotic effects of the fictional dream is that fiction has a great deal of influence on the reader, who models himself on heroic characters or takes up behaviours and value systems and attitudes displayed by fictional heroes and heroines. Such effects can be harmful. "One way of undermining fiction's harmful effects is the writing of metafiction," Gardner says, "a story that calls attention to its methods and shows the reader what is happening to him as he reads" (87). In other words, the fiction shows how it is put together, and that it is an artifice and not reality.

What Gardner is talking about, and what many critics of so-called postmodernism in fiction are missing, is that the genre of the novel has built into itself the constant ability to change and to take on any other kind of text, genre, or discourse, without ceasing to be a novel or novelistic fiction. This placement of the novel as a genre is explained most exhaustively by Mikhail Bakhtin in his essays collected under the title *The Dialogic Imagination*. Bakhtin set out to describe the difference between the novel and all other genres, and concluded that the only genre that is absolutely flexible and that has no boundaries or generic closure is the novel. One may not only insert into novelistic fiction any other kind of textual discourse or documentary language, but one may do so with an unlimited number of voices and points of view, and still not have left the novel behind. Bakhtin describes the novel as a free-for-all genre, which would make the above criticisms of what constitutes "irregular" fictional activity absurd. Bakhtin writes at length in "Epic and Novel" about "this ability of the novel to criticize itself" (4), which is what "metafiction" is for. The emphasis is on the unpredictability of the genre, and that "the novel is the only developing genre and therefore it reflects more deeply, more essentially, more sensitively and rapidly, reality itself in the process of its unfolding...it best of all reflects the tendencies of a new world still in the making; it is, after all, the only genre born of this new world and in total affinity with it" (7).

Writing metafiction is therefore a revolutionary stance in writing—a way of countering the narcotic effect of the continually created mythologies that enable society to carry on its mass neuroses and traditions. In metafiction, "the breaks in the dream are as important as the dream," Gardner notes (87). Insofar as metafictional writing, and deconstruction, investigates language and the uses of language, the demythologizing practice of theory-fiction has a certain social and intellectual value. Gardner points out that "behind the deconstructionists' dazzling cloud of language lie certain more or less indisputable facts: that language carries values with it, sometimes values we do not recognize as we speak and would not subscribe to if we noticed their presence in what we say; and that art (music, painting, literature, etc.) is language" (88). The important point for Gardner is "that language carries values is obvious" (88). In response to those values, many of which are retrograde and out of keeping with the times, "deconstruction is the practice of taking language apart, or taking works of art apart, to discover their unacknowledged inner workings" (88). Since all good literature involves itself in some kind of investigation, Gardner points out that "all great literature has, to some extent, a deconstructive impulse" (89). Further, "the smart writer of metafictions is selective about what he pokes fun at, and part of our interest as we read his work comes from our recognition that the folly he points out is significant; that is, it is not only silly once we look at it closely, but it is in some sense perverse: it pushes wrong values" (92).

One of the novelist's biggest concerns, and which has bearing on the deconstruction of the fictional dream, is memory: the uses of memory, the way in which memory appears to us. The postmodern writer is concerned with the self-mythologizing we engage in, and the combined sense of past time and loss that is involved in memory. We often refer to Proust when talking about memory, and the idea of an unwilling memory flow: the place that visits us, rather than we it; the concept of memory time and memory space which is disconnected from real time and space. We distinguish between memory time and real time: time in our memories is like a dream wherein all things can happen simultaneously and experiences are subjective; "real" time is when things happen in a certain order and are collectively experienced and ascertained. The world out there is something separate from the world in here, although in modernism much effort has gone into uniting the two. Postmodern writing, however, does not observe that separation between dream and reality, the subjective and objective—does not observe binaries in general—and has a way of engaging much more than personal memory, dream time, experience, and loss. This kind of writing also uses other texts, sometimes in order to expand on the idea of memory, and engage communal memory in the personal sphere. Because cultural memory is lodged in books, postmodern writing works with theory and mixes discourses to such an extent that the reader's expectations are confused. That confusion is central to what a postmodern work is all about. Certitude itself is part of what is being questioned.

Robert Kroetsch, one of Canada's foremost postmodernist writers, has shown how the various elements of personal autobiography, memory, communal mythologies, history and history-making, writing and forgetfulness, the blank page and the text, the margin and the centre, all come together in a postmodern text. The writer of such a work has to acknowledge that he cannot really tell a brand new story, and he cannot actually say anything original. However, the fact that writing derives from other writing is neither good nor bad. The acceptance of the derivative nature of writing conditions us toward a form of humility, which is far more poetic and human than the arrogance we associate with the idea of originality. Kroetsch's collection of essays *A Likely Story*, shows what the attitude of a postmodern writer is bound to be. He melds various genres to make up essays of all kinds in this book, and he uses both storytelling and poetry as well as more specialized essayistic formats all at once. One could say that in doing so, Kroetsch has "novelized" the essay, to use Bakhtin's term. But Kroetsch goes to the limit with the idea of theory-fiction and problems of originality. For example, in his essay "Lonesome Writer Diptych," which is also a poem, Kroetsch suggests that even autobiography is derivative. He writes that "by borrowing fragments of other lives I borrow an autobiography of my own" (117-18). And in another essay on "Sitting Down to Write: Margaret Laurence and the Discourse of Morning," he states flatly that "the chances of being original are less than slim. They don't exist" (151).[3]

For the critics of postmodernism, theory has no place in fiction. While metafiction, when the narrator intervenes in the story he is telling and comments on how it is going, has been an acceptable element of fiction since at least the days of Fielding's *Tom Jones* and Sterne's *Tristram Shandy*, it is a different matter when the intrusive voice is a theorizing one, and when it begins to deliver textual analysis and literary criticism along with cultural and linguistic theory. That is seen as pompous, perhaps, although it's all right if the intrusive narrator talks about all manner of other things. As a response to the criticism that literary theory is destructive to the novel when inserted into it, I want to refer to an essay by Hélène Cixous called "The School of the Dead."[4]

"The School of the Dead" is about the strange "science" of writing—what goes into writing, and what comes out of it. Cixous contends that writing bridges the two worlds of life and death. Writing speaks two languages. But written works do not appear and exist in a vacuum. There are ancestors and descendants to texts. Writing in the first place involves obeying a kind of call (*Three Steps* 5). The question is, whose call? Perhaps the answer is the call of the dead, Cixous suggests, or the call of the past and all the books it has left behind. Writing is an apprenticeship. Cixous does not just mean the writer apprenticing other writers, but texts apprenticing each other. If a text is an apprenticeship to other texts, it would be natural for it to reflect its influences, to make them transparent and to show a certain self-consciousness about its own genesis and process. In doing so, the writer can acknowledge a dept that is owing. Such acknowledgements could move us closer to "honest" writing, if the mechanisms involved are shown for what they are.

The idea of indebtedness and of accepting that indebtedness comes out in Paul Auster's interview with Edmond Jabès. Jabès says there that "in all my books there is a book that exists inside the book...The book creates itself, against all the other books we carry inside us" (Auster 153). Jabès is ostensibly talking about *The Book of Questions,* a fragmented story without traditional composition. But in his reflections, there is an aesthetic that is necessary for the fragmented time in which such a work operates. That aesthetic is spoken of by Jabès in the following way: "as the text advances, there are things that come from farther and farther away, as if from another book, or from the book within the book" (154). The writer has, in reality, a never-ending debt that he wishes to acknowledge. "There is always a book carrying a book carrying a book carrying a book" he says, as if any given text were composed of a series of endlessly pregnant texts (154).

Perhaps theory-fiction, the book that has other books inside it, is about not lying.[5] Postmodern writing presumably cannot lie because its function in the first place is to help us see what we spend most of our lives not seeing, to make apparent what we obliterate in the course of living. We fictionalize, we deny, we rationalize, we mythologize, we create order where there is none. Metafictional and postmodernist writing is about not forgetting the variegated universe we exist in. No single, unified, coherent story will tell the "truth," although it may be a good story. Such writing is also an enactment of memory and a reinstatement of lives not lived. Says Cixous in *Three Steps on the Ladder of Writing,* "writing, in its noblest function, is the attempt to unease, to unearth, to find the primitive picture again, ours, the one that frightens us" (9). But this is not about confessional or trauma literature, where the writer explores her own emotions and unearths personal psychologies, confusing writing with therapy. To explore "what frightens us" can be seen as a more communal enterprise. It is to write what frightens the community. And for that we need the presence of all those other texts.

Cixous is talking about the relationship we have to what has passed: to the past, to history. She means that writing originates in what is contrary. It may seem simple to erase the past by ignoring it. It is harder to acknowledge what came before—without distorting it and remaking history in another image, something frequently done in politics.

Acknowledging something requires knowing it in the first place. Having acquainted ourselves with events, ideas, and texts, it is also a challenge to superimpose what we know onto the present and ourselves. It becomes the writer's task to carry on traditions of thought, engage them, refine them, and re-enact them. In opposition to that, it seems a solipsistic gesture to pretend all our ideas are our own and claim possession of what we have found. To Cixous, extreme though the thought is, the unwillingness to live or to write in that shared space amounts to a form of murder.

"Beneath this book there are hundreds of books that weren't written" Cixous claims (*Three Steps* 15). By this she means that the book you write or the book that appears is only the version of the text that has survived. There are numerous other versions you might have written that have not survived. Similarly, beneath each book there are hundreds of books that were written. As Edmond Jabès says, "the book carries all books within itself" (Auster 164). These are books that have appeared, and which exist in the present book as ghosts until they are acknowledged. The presence of all those other books in any given book is inevitable, since, in Jabès's words, "behind each word other words are hiding" (Auster 168). Words themselves are haunted. Jabès's metaphor for this phenomenon is the sea:

> I think of this in terms of the sea, in the image of the sea as it breaks upon the shore. It is not the wave that comes. It is the whole sea that comes each time and the whole sea that draws back. It is never just a wave, it is always everything that comes and everything that goes. (Auster 169)

Acknowledging that haunting in what you write becomes important, not just for the life of ideas in a community, but also for the sake of history. In talking about Ingeborg Bachmann, for example, Cixous explores the idea of what she calls "the virus of crime" (*Three Steps* 19). The virus of crime continues to exist. The massacres of history are not necessarily things of the past. She quotes Bachmann's notion that "the assassins are still among us," even though the particular war she was talking about, fascism, anti-Semitism, the Holocaust, was ostensibly over (19). Bachmann contends that "everything is war. War doesn't begin with the first bombs that are dropped" (19). We need to constantly read what the community writes in order to discover where we are positioned in the ideological wars of our time. Engaging the texts of the community inside your text is a way of clarifying our relation-

We must eliminate war, or thoughts of war in our minds.

61

ships to each other's thoughts and disabusing ourselves of our ideological and intellectual delusions.

The idea of engaging or incorporating history and the texts that have already appeared (which narrate and comment on that history) does not have to happen in coherent or scholarly ways in fiction-theory. This is not about writing history or promoting master narratives. Often the idea of post-structuralism involves a kind of deconstruction which does the exact opposite of history. But deconstructing past texts is not a new phenomenon. Quoting in order to dislodge texts from contexts is already as old as modernism itself. An early example of quotationism in the novel, for example, is James Joyce's *A Portrait of the Artist as a Young Man.* This novel is filled with quotes from poems, verses, sermons, prayers, and so on. Seamus Deane, who edited the Joyce works for Penguin Books, points out that in this novel, "quotations are so numerous that they entirely take over the text," and "the ratio of ten quotations to a dozen pages is at least sustained and often exceeded" (xvi). Deane notes that for Joyce, quotationism is a political act, and a way of taking over the past. In his words, "for in quotation they [quotes] undergo a torsion that wrenches them from their own context and replaces them in the context of the writer who quotes" (xx).

To wrench quotes from their context and reposition them in another light is also a way of repositioning logic itself. Hence, we have the Dadaists. Paul Auster, in his essay on Hugo Ball, one of the founders of Dada, explains how Dada might be seen as a precursor to postmodernism. Dada tries to overturn all systems of logic. The confusions inherent in conflicted moments of history, and the position of the artist inside those moments, are forefronted. Because the artist, or the writer, falls between disciplines, the only honest thing a writer can do is mix the disciplines and show the meshings. About Hugo Ball himself, Auster argues that he was "too much an artist to be a philosopher, too much a philosopher to be an artist, too concerned with the fate of the world to think only in terms of personal salvation, and yet too inward to be an effective activist" (55). It is the writer's condition and fate to be a little of everything.

One good example of an early variant of intellectual dislocation is the "quotationist" Walter Benjamin, for whom it was an objective to actually construct texts that were made up of nothing but quotations from other texts. Walter Benjamin was a German-Jewish expatriate living in Paris, who died in 1940. He was part of the intelligentsia of his time, but while admired by his peers, he was not widely published.

He persisted in writing essays and criticism that fell outside of common practice. Using quotations elaborately was one of his unusual methods. His reasoning was that he shared with his modernist peers the conviction that all traditions and cultures should be questioned, and the whole idea of "belonging" to a culture or a tribe or group was thrown into doubt by the times. According to Hannah Arendt, European intellectuals, especially those of Jewish background, "looked upon the dawn of a new age basically as a decline and viewed history along with the traditions which led up to this decline as a field of ruins" (37). This is precisely the view of contemporary cross-currents that so-called postmodernists of the late twentieth century espouse, and the development of postmodernism out of early modernism seems consistent.

The relationship between the view of history as a "field of ruins" and the uses of quotations, and incorporating theory into fictional narratives (as well as non-fictional ones) becomes reasonable when looking at someone like Walter Benjamin. Benjamin wanted to lose the idea of authority. If the master narrative gets scrambled, the idea of authority is lost. Instead of bowing to tradition and the authority of the past, the writer has to find another way of dealing with the debris that has come down to us. Benjamin thought of his extracontextual quoting as a "modern" way of using past texts. His idea was to "tear [texts] out of context" and thereby "destroy" them (39). In his view, the only way the past could survive was if the good nuggets were torn out of the fabric of history. It is like scanning the ocean for pearls and removing them. In Arendt's words, "the past spoke directly only through things that had not been handed down, whose seeming closeness to the present was thus due precisely to their exotic character, which ruled out all claims to a binding authority" (40). With this line of thinking, when a narrative includes quotations from theory, or cites theory, the author is not necessarily succumbing to the authority of that theorist or that idea, but is in fact deconstructing the theory, destroying the commentary, at the same time as she is interrupting the narrative. This is partly in order to undo the idea that there is an authority anywhere on anything. Like Benjamin, the quotationist wishes to "break the spell of tradition" simply because it is a spell (Arendt 42). Also, the past needs to be interpreted "with 'the deadly impact' of new thoughts" (46).

Without such a break in tradition's spell, there is an unfortunate way, it has been argued, in which the perfect, seamless novels we recognize as flawless narratives actually participate in the fascism of their time. Epic, narrativistic novels sometimes serve to carry on the status quo and uphold the power structures that exist—even when they think they do not. This happens when the language of those narratives remains unexamined, when connotations and associations are allowed to act out their clichéd existence. We can be hypnotized by a smooth unbroken narrative into thinking that things are in order, even when the story we are reading is about disorder. So many of our conscientious writers, however, have been reminding us of the dangers of the unexamined fiction. Conscientious writing never takes its own language for granted, nor its own ideas. The seamless narrative, however, acts as a pacifier for the reader who does not need to interact with the text. The distancing dimension of, for example, third-person narratives, well-formed plots, and smooth standard language makes it possible for the reader not to have to believe, not to be touched fundamentally. Literature can become an opiate. To avoid literature serving as a kind of inducement to narcosis, we can qualify our descriptions, make strange the ordinary, fragment narrative texture. We can produce unexpected intimacies, allow for authorial intervention, open up avenues of interaction between the fiction itself and the real world in which it exists.

Theorized writing is about interrogating the present: about intervening in current textual practices, about resisting the kind of canonization that society sanctions and the market economy encourages. Such writing interferes with ideas and habits and practices that are forced on us, until we no longer remember what we thought about things—until we forget there are counter-ideas. We need the constant reminder that there are other peoples, other cultures, other languages, and that the hegemony of our own literary culture can be examined— that ours are not the absolute methods and solutions. The choice theory-fiction makes is to opt for multiplicity and multivalency at the expense of ease and comfort. Postmodernism looks for a kind of dialogic in the face of the monologue imposed on us. It is dialogical writing that takes into account the other voices in the community and interacts with them, even at the time of writing. After all, the whole idea of culture in the West is rendered suspect by its history. To quote André Brink, from his essay "The Languages of Culture," Western "culture was the prerogative of the aristocracy, to be emulated later, in the wake of the French Revolution, by the bourgeoisie" (226). Given this fact, Brink continues, "how can it [culture] be regarded—at least by the Third World—other than with suspicion, doubt, or open rejection?" (226). It is no longer possible to assume our cultural codes are intact, and can or should be transmitted in a package. Introducing theoretical metafiction into imaginative literature is one way of disassembling the context which is suspect anyway, and remaking it.

There is an extra impetus for the inclusion of theory in fiction for the woman writer. There is a certain pressure imposed on women writers, that their work be "moving," emotional, and therefore that it should exclude the intellect. It is harder, in other words, to be accepted if what you do is intellectual, because that is not expected of you if you are a woman. However, engaging the intellect along with the poetic is a healthy thing to do. Why would you not want to engage the whole mind, all parts of it, rather than just your emotions? It would be like having a large vocabulary at your disposal but using only a few words of it. It is unnecessary to see a discrepancy, or even a division, between what we know as academic and what we think of as creative writing. There is no good reason to compartmentalize like that. Such parcelling out of our experience with language is another way of colluding with the power structure—the one that safeguards academic activity within highly exclusive structures. Focusing on emotions to the exclusion of ideas and theories becomes a trap for the woman writer, whereas postmodernist methods present her with a way out of that prison. The invitation to write postmodernistically is a way to escape the predetermined strictures that will face the woman writer at all the checkpoints of her writing career: whether her book is published, what the critics say, how the book is marketed, and the validation of her work.

The point to be made here is that the writing of postmodernist fiction, theory-laden narratives, conglomerates of quotations, and notes that take the place of master narratives which exude authority and order, is not necessarily an academic venture. Much of the criticism of such "experimental" writing concerns its so-called academic elitism. But writers everywhere practise these disorienting forms of literature. One early example of a writer who was not academic and who came on her own version of the subterfuge text very naturally was Laura Riding. Paul Auster's description of Riding's book *The Telling* explains. *The Telling*, he writes,

> fits into no established literary category [and] is positively Talmudic in structure. *The Telling* itself is a short text of less than fifty pages, divided into numbered paragraphs, originally written for an issue of the magazine *Chelsey* in 1967. To this "core-text" which is written in a dense, highly abstract prose almost totally devoid of outside references, she has added a series of commentaries, commentaries

on commentaries, notes and addenda, which flesh out many of the
earlier conclusions and treat of various literary, political, and philosophical matters. (69-70)

More than this, Auster finds that this text by Riding is "an astonishing
display of a consciousness confronting and examining itself" (70). That
confrontation and examination is what theory-fiction is all about.

Paul Auster has written many commentaries and reviews of Jewish
writers in an effort to both examine and display the particular nexus
that describes the condition of the Jewish author in the twentieth century. Much of that material turns out to be postmodern in nature, for
reasons which are clearly defined and understood by the writers themselves. Yet these are not academic ventures, and a case is clearly made
that something in what we think of as postmodernism, the blending of
discourses and fragmentation of narratives, answers to the conditions
of the times. That may be one reason why Auster is particularly intrigued
by Edmond Jabès, whose _The Book of Questions_ he describes in these
words:

> Jabès has created a new and mysterious kind of literary work—as
> dazzling as it is difficult to define. Neither novel nor poem, neither
> essay nor play, _The Book of Questions_ is a combination of all these
> forms, a mosaic of fragments, aphorisms, dialogues, songs, and com-
> mentaries that endlessly move around the central question of the
> book: how to speak what cannot be spoken. (107)

Auster conflates the Holocaust and "the question of literature itself"
when talking about Jabès, because the Holocaust defines, identifies, and
highlights the complete collapse of narrative possibilities in the second
half of the twentieth century. Writers who are conscious have to respond
to that collapse. In the words of Maurice Blanchot, commenting on Jabès,
Jabès's writing "must be accomplished in the act of interrupting itself"
(in Auster 111). It is the interruptions that prevent a narrative from becoming the kind of "fascistic" attempt at "mastery" which we associate with
the seamless text—the kind of good old-fashioned novel hailed by Laura
Miller in the _New York Times_. Part of the impetus of such interruptions
is to make sure "the reader's eye can never grow accustomed to a single,
unbroken visual field," writes Auster. "One reads the book by fits and
starts—just as it was written" (111).

What is being proposed here by theory-fiction, or post-structuralist,
multivalent fiction, is akin to what Julia Kristeva calls "textual practice."
In her book _Revolution in Poetic Language_, Kristeva categorizes four

types of linguistic usage, or textual politics. One is narrative; another is contemplative language; a third is academic discourse; and a fourth is textual practice. The last of these in fact engages the other three. Textual practice is not about story (the family); it is not about lyricism or contemplation (poetry); it is not academic (exclusion of the subject and narrative). Instead it is about process. Textual practice is about engaging the entire semiotic life of the writer, and of employing the subjective along with depersonalized discourses. Textual practice creates itself as it moves on. It is a language and a textual mode that is alive. Writing as textual practice is an entirely different process from the forms of writing we have known, which have created the genres we recognize, and which are still winning the prizes in the literary marketplace. The process of textual practice involves all of the writer, at all levels, and all the linguistic and sublinguistic engagements the writer is capable of.

Textual practice contains the act of theory-fiction, which is only one of many ways of incorporating a multitude of discourses at once. Multiplicities, multivalencies, multiple discourses: writing that involves as many levels as possible is closer to the whole of our semiotic experience, and therefore engages the reader and the writer to a greater extent, than uniform, unilingual tracts are able to. Such engagements include both memory and the breath that is presently being drawn; both the past and the present, the subjective and the objective, the theoretical and the experiential, all at once.

This is not to collapse all distinction between metafiction, fictionalized theory, hyperfiction, post-structuralism, postmodernism, and textual practice. These are not the same thing in different words. But it takes a longer treatise than is possible here to elaborate on those differences. Instead, it is the core these practices have in common that is of interest here. As to hyperfiction, which is the narrative form with which this essay opened: the claims made for it, to which the essayist in the *Review* was answering, are overcharged to begin with. The argument presented by Miller concerning the advent of hyperfiction is overwrought. However, hyperfiction may well find its way into future reading habits through no fault of the so-called post-structuralists. Simply put, technology invents its own forms, and the Internet is a study in hyperfiction all by itself. The genre of the novel, moreover, as Bakhtin has amply explained, allows for any new form brought on by any new type of technology. As Botswanan writer Bessie Head says in her essay "Some Notes on Novel Writing," included in her book

*A Woman Alone,* "I have found that the novel form is like a large rag-bag into which one can stuff anything—all one's philosophical, social and romantic speculations" (64). Further, echoing Bakhtin and the sense that the novel is a forward-looking, future-driven, "genre," Head confesses that "I have always reserved a special category for myself, as a writer—that of a pioneer blazing a new trail into the future" (64). The presence of theory, like the presence of philosophy or intertextuality, is not a straw man that needs to be taken down. On the contrary, theory-charged fiction, or fictionalized theory, is another way of telling a story, and as argued here, often a truer, cleaner, more honest (if more messy) way of being face to face with the narrative act and its relation to history, both private and communal.

*... and why not?*

# 6 | Writing and Silence
## The Unteachable Mystery of Words

Our relationship to writing and to texts is sometimes precarious and often confused. We have become uncertain of the nature and location of literature and the arts, about the placement of the subject, ourselves, in language and in narrative. For those who teach writing, whether literary or not, the issues often become murky. The writing teacher is caught in the peculiar position of having to teach something he or she suspects cannot be taught. Everything about writing becomes an approximation. How is this so? And how do we comport ourselves in light of our difficulties, when we live in such a text-based society? Where everything important happens in writing? Legal documents, legislation, educational degrees and diplomas, school essays? We suspect, along with Eudora Welty writing in *The Eye of the Story*, that "there is no explanation outside fiction for what its writer is learning to do" (110). Welty found herself trying to explain the unexplainable in her various essays on the writing act, and like many other writers, ended up with ironies. Welty's explanation for the mysteriousness of the writing process has its roots in the notion that whenever a writer sits down to tell a story in writing, she is experimenting. Every act of imaginative writing is an exploration into the unknown (Welty 110). As if to echo Welty, Bessie Head asserts in an essay on South African writing from 1979, that "the main function of a writer is to make life magical and to communicate a sense of wonder" (67).

In his book *Writing Degree Zero*, Roland Barthes proposes a more scientific explanation when he describes what appears to him to be our relationship to three aspects of verbal communication: language, style, and writing. Language is the speech we use, he explains—what we say every day and what is said to us. Language is the spoken word that reverberates according to our special time and place in history. Style is what we are: what is inside us. Style is our passions, our desires, loves, and rages. Our bodies, culture, and personal histories go into

*Notes to chapter 6 are on p. 112.*

making our style. We cannot alter or control it any more than we can alter our deepest psyches. Finally, writing is a kind of ritual. Writing is a ceremony we participate in, with its own rules and conditions, its own history and culture. We enter a kind of "templum" when we write, and we are no longer ourselves.

Inside the temple of writing, we have further ritualized what we think of as literature. We have a dislocated relationship to non-literature, but a much more ceremonialized relationship to so-called literary writing. In this connection, it is worth mentioning an essay by Maurice Blanchot on Antonin Artaud, simply called "Artaud," which appeared in the 1996 edition of *The Blanchot Reader*.[1] Here Blanchot tells the story of Artaud's correspondence with the editor Jacques Rivière. At twenty-seven, Artaud sent some poems to a journal and got them returned rejected. The young poet wrote back and asked what was wrong with the poems, that he couldn't think and couldn't write and needed to know. A correspondence ensued about speechlessness and thinker's block, which became so interesting after awhile to Rivière, that he asked if he could publish the correspondence instead. Artaud said he could if he also published some of the poems, so in the end some of the original poems were published, but in the context of the correspondence. It was the discussion about the writing that was interesting—where the dynamism and energy of Artaud's thinking lay.

This story is interesting for several reasons. For one, what would it be about the young poet that makes him unable to express himself in literature (poetry), but perfectly articulate in his epistolary writing? Only if he can say what he has to say in poetry will the poet be content, and it is only in poetry that he fails and is tongue-tied. The story also illustrates the strained relationship we have with literature, literary writing, as opposed to non-literary writing. While discussing this subject, Blanchot also mentions Marcel Proust, who spent a long time writing letters to people as a kind of preparation for the writing of his great work *Remembrance of Things Past*. Writing letters for Proust, "so many letters" to "so many people," constituted his approach to literature itself. Those metatexts (the letters, which talk about writing while writing) turn out to be necessary marginalia in the history of Proust's great work—and in the history of literature in general.

Blanchot's objective with these stories is to focus our sense of what literature actually is. He wrote a series of essays in 1953 ("The Disappearance of Literature"; "The Pursuit of the Zero Point"; and "The Death of the Last Writer") where he argues against the stagnant notion that had grown around the idea of literary or artistic writing and the product-oriented culture of literary works. He shifts all the emphasis from product to process: what goes into the writing itself, rather than what happens to the book afterwards. Once he has focused on the process, the effect is much more mysterious and less predictable. The writer at work becomes a person engaged in something almost mystical; something, he says, which is "incomprehensible to almost everyone" else ("Disappearance," *Reader* 137). The writing act is a region of experience that is beyond the grasp of the general culture, he says.

Insofar as poetic writing is "mysterious" in an "incomprehensible" way, there are many takes on what is involved in that mystery. One of the mysteries is the relationship between the imaginative text and silence. James Tate, a Pulitzer Prize-winning American poet, puts the essential idea of this mystery in terms of a kind of haunting, when he discusses these things in an essay titled "Live Yak Pie," which appeared in *Best American Poetry of 1997*, and which was republished in his book *The Route as Briefed*. Tate argues that "poetry speaks against an essential backdrop of silence. It is almost reluctant to speak at all, knowing that it can never fully name what is at the heart of its intention. There is a prayerful, haunted silence between words, between phrases, between images, ideas, and lines" (4). The poem gives us a glance at "the other world," which is otherwise inaccessible to us. Tate says that "the reader, perhaps without knowing it, instinctively desires to peer between the cracks into the other world where the unspoken rests in darkness" (4).

James Tate takes the idea of the "unspoken" in a poem further still in a lecture he gave at Ohio University in 1995, which was published as "Tatters of the *Morpho* Butterfly" in 1999. Tate is here talking about what he calls "the shadow poem," which is the poem behind the poem—that which the poem is not saying, but which may still be "read" there. He believes that "if it is a good poem, there will always be an element that cannot be explained" (133). That element is "what we might call 'the shadow poem,' The poem we read says it is doing one thing, is about such and such, when really the important work, the real work, is being done offstage, as it were" (135). An element of innuendo and deceptiveness enters in the creation of the "shadow text." This the poet does because he wishes to get in touch with that which is most mysterious in the human mind:

And why would a poet want to work this way in the employment of deception creating shadow poems? Because it is a difficult busi-

ness, being intensely conscious of all the ways the poem is working, and simultaneously hoping, nay, counting on, breaking into
the vaults of the unconscious where valuable documents and price-
less jewels are stored. And yet this is what we do. (137)

Just because the mystery has here the name of the "unconscious" does
not make it less of a mystery. The poet knows that "so much takes place
in the labyrinths of the mind, so many wonders and surprises and mon-
strosities" (142). Where Antonin Artaud stumbled, when as a young
man he tried to publish poems that were not working for him, but
which he could discuss in letters, is precisely here in the creation of
the "shadow poem." The shadow poem makes us stumble. It is difficult
and unknowable.

Maurice Blanchot would argue that we do not know what literature
is. We are wrong in our thinking that certain works are literary while others are not, without knowing anything about what went into them. He
would say that the so-called masterworks we associate with literary
classics are not literature at all, but rather products designed to perpet-
uate themselves. That is, classical writings are accepted as masterful
precisely because they do no harm to the culture that endorses them, and
they do not place literature itself at risk. As if to endorse Blanchot's
view of classical literature, Jorge Luis Borges proposed his definition of
a classic in 1977. The word *classic*, according to Borges, "comes from
*classis*: a frigate, a fleet. A classic book is a well-run book; everything must
be on board it" (95). A well-run ship will not be at risk of sinking. True
literature however, in Blanchot's view, does put both itself, its own language, and the culture from which it springs, at significant risk. True literature is always in danger of destroying itself. The process involved in
real creativity is dangerous and even self-obliterating.

In "The Pursuit of the Zero Point," Blanchot further argues that
the artistic sensibility and mode of expression are not necessary for
today's pursuit of knowledge. The fact that art is not considered necessary by the mainstream culture gives it a marginal status, which
also renders it safe for consumption. What attracts writers to writing in modern times, it seems to him, is the feeling that you can do
and say everything in art. There is boundless possibility and freedom
there. But he points out the obvious, which is that everything is
really nothing. What the real writer aims to reach is a kind of neutrality he calls "degree zero," where none of the ambitious factors
connected to art production matter. Ultimately, true writing reaches
for its end in silence.

In "The Death of the Last Writer," written two years later, Blanchot argues that the writing he has in mind will act as an ultimate silencer. In the noise and cacophonous speech in which we live, the true utterance is experienced as the word that silences all the words. Literature is, in his words, a "rich dwelling place of silence" (152). It is here Blanchot appears at his most mystical and paradoxical. He speaks of the enemy within; the empty mirror; the foreign voice; the voice that imitates the writer's own voice; the speech of the wilderness—all of these are what haunts the writer at work. What he means by such metaphors is, like the writing endeavour itself, almost too obscure. The true creative artist will recognize the dislocations involved in the writing act: the movement that makes your own voice sound foreign; that takes away your own reflection when you look in the mirror; that utters from a centre you did not acknowledge and that is your enemy; the sense that you are coming from a great wilderness. For most other people, these sensibilities are simply not there.

Many of the ideas lodged in Blanchot's essays resurface in Paul Auster's more recent discussions on Samuel Beckett. Beckett was coming out of cultural crystallizations similar to Blanchot's, and at the same time in history. Auster notes some features of Beckett that also pertain to Blanchot. Beckett wrote plotless texts, stories that went nowhere, either in fictional or dramatic form. "Nothing happens. Or, more precisely, what happens is what does not happen," Auster explains (84). Further, as if to underline the notion that writing emerges from silence and then silences itself, Auster says that in Beckett's writing, "whatever is said is said at the very moment there is nothing left to say" (86). Imaginative, poetic writing is inherently contradictory—a paradoxical enterprise. "The key word in all this," Auster notes, "is dispossession. Beckett, who begins with little, ends with even less. The movement in each of his works is toward a kind of unburdening, by which he leads us to the limits of experience" (87). The "limit of experience" is a place of mystery and, ultimately, not really communicable.

In his essay on Paul Celan, Auster discusses a more intense version of the unspeakableness of poetic language and its border of silence. Paul Celan, a Jew who survived the Holocaust and started writing after it, wrote out of painful memory. He never wrote about anything else. Such a memory is unspeakable, and much has been written (for example by Theodor Adorno and Primo Levi) about the difficulty of writing about one's own trauma. About this phenomenon—of needing to write about what cannot be articulated—Auster claims that "the unspeakable yields a poetry that continually threatens to overwhelm the limits of what can be spoken" (91). The contradiction here lies in the soldering together of unforgettable memory and the unspeakable silence it gives rise to. Because of the relationship between writing and memory in Paul Celan's case, Auster points out what many other writers attest to: that sometimes writing is a necessity, not a choice. And "it is this feeling of necessity that communicates itself to a reader," Auster says of Celan, whose poems "are more than literary artifacts. They are a means of staying alive" (96). The effect of such an intense relationship to writing makes it impossible for someone like Celan to move beyond that space, as it is for Beckett. As Auster puts it, "Celan's poetry is continually collapsing into itself, negating its very premises, again and again arriving at zero" (97).

Maurice Blanchot's essays are, similarly, also significant in their severe contradictoriness. The power of Blanchot's arguments tends to come from the irony of his phraseology: literature appears only at the moment it is disappearing; the writer's word occurs only to silence all words. Paradoxes of this nature abound. Others have perhaps articulated more precisely what is meant by the concept of neutrality as it relates to writing, such as Roland Barthes, whose idea of the "text of bliss" may better illustrate the point at which art and intellect part company. But Blanchot's thoughts are mentioned here because they speak of something that is not often present in discussions about writing, and which it might be valuable to remember. That is, that there is something mysterious in the act of writing. There is something contemplative to the experience of putting words on the page in the exercise of one's imagination, which people who do not engage in are hard pressed to understand. That seemingly mysterious and contemplative component of writing relates to a comment Auster has made about Celan's poetry. Auster says that Celan "does not mention anything directly, but weaves his meanings into the fabric of the language, creating a space for the invisible, in the same way that thought accompanies us as we move through a landscape" (99). What the poet has to say cannot be said directly, so it is left to intimation. It is perhaps this element in creative writing that drives writers mad, like Ernest Hemingway; drives them to hospitals, like Tennessee Williams; drives them to suicide, like Virginia Woolf; drives them to silence, like Kate Chopin.

Hélène Cixous has talked about these same ideas as Blanchot and Auster in her book *Coming to Writing*. The writing act can be engaged in, she claims, only when the writer has lost all ties to the phenomenological world and is fully involved in the spiritual. The fears that have to be lost, she says, are "the fear of reaching joy, acute joy, the fear of allowing oneself to be carried away by exaltation, fear of adoring" (121). The artistic pursuit has in it the mystical elements of exaltation and adoration. These are passions that cannot be transmitted, but come from inside the artist, like faith itself. Note this declaration of the ecstatic nature of art, when Cixous is talking about painting. The painter, she says, "gives himself to painting as others do to God. And as the dead man does to science. So that it can advance on his body" (*Coming* 125).

The same tie between the written word, the writing act, and faith and adoration, is spoken of by Jorge Luis Borges as well. In his essay on "The Kabbalah," Borges tries to account for the nature of scripture, or the sacred book. In his view, the sacred book is significantly different from the classic book. The classic book is grounded in everything we know, but the sacred book emanates from magical culture, which has its origins in something we do not know. Speaking of the Koran as "the prototype of the magical book," Borges claims it is a Muslim belief that the Koran "is a book—this is incredible, but this is how it is—that is older than the Arabic language" (97). The word here existed before it was ever uttered. He explains that "For the orthodox Moslems the Koran is an attribute of God, like His rage, His pity, or His justice" (97). These comments serve to remind us that the idea of language as sacred, and writing as magical, has always been with us, but has become somewhat eclipsed in the twentieth century. Maurice Blanchot, I believe, was trying to shift some of the emphasis back to the sacred from the profane, in order to say something essential about the nature of the writing act.

Inherent in Maurice Blanchot's arguments is what has come to be known as process writing. This is a way of looking at writing not as product, but as an act constantly in development. Writing writes itself. One idea flows from another, one phrase from another, with a life of its own that has more to do with language and semiotics than with the will of the writer. And the writing is alive only for as long as it is being written. Once on the page, the text is dead. What Julia Kristeva calls textual practice is part of this way of seeing writing. Textual practice brings to bear on the act of writing everything the writer, the language, the culture, the moment of history, the geographical location in which the act takes place, all are. It is an entirely different thing to view writing simply as the production of texts which get put to academic or commercial use. For Blanchot, writing becomes literature only when it is alive with process, and not dead as a marketable text.

In his essay "The Great Hoax" from 1958, Blachot uses Roland Barthes's book *Mythologies* as a springboard for further reflections on what amounts to the mysteries of the writing act. Barthes collected columns written over time for the magazine industry, where he takes various items, objects, and incidents from everyday life and discusses their real import, their true value, and their mythological dimensions. Everything in the world, Barthes argues, is subject to mythological scrutiny of this kind. Nothing is exempt. As Blanchot says, there is no such thing as specialized knowledge when it comes to cultural analysis. But the disappearance of specialized knowledge, and the appearance of another set of signs and symbols with which to discuss what we thought we already knew, is the prerogative of the writer. That is what writing is about.

In short, we use the language we have at our disposal to exchange supposedly neutral facts and information. However, underneath this official language is another language: the language of myth. Everything we see has a truer import on the mythological level. There is a mythological meaning to everything. Blanchot leads into his discussion of mythologies by talking about what he calls "the great hoax." Everything is seen by human nature as conspiratorial, the thinking goes—there is a hidden agenda behind everything that is said and done in human affairs. Our sense of the conspiratorial goes so far as to ascribe hidden designs to God and even to nature. Certainly when we get to Marxism and Freudianism, psychoanalysis and historicized socialism, we find our conspiracy theories acquire new, structural and socio-historical form, rendering them even more acceptable. We see ourselves as victims in an elaborate, universal hoax, Blanchot claims. Our task, in light of this, is to see through the surface into the conspiracies underneath. To unearth the hidden agendas. We derive pleasure, he says, from our identification as victims, simply because that makes us innocent.

That view of the world as essentially deceiving in its appearances, and hostile underneath, is brought into language and writing by our capacity to mythologize. Myth-making is more or less the act of unearthing the hoax, the hidden agenda underneath everything. While such views may seem psychologically obsessive, they make sense when it comes to language. As a matter of fact, we do communicate information on the one hand, but mean a lot more with it on the other. Barthes's example, repeated by Blanchot, serves to illustrate this argument. Barthes describes a recruitment poster for the French army, showing a black soldier in a French uniform saluting the French flag. On the one hand, the poster simply shows a soldier in the act of being a soldier, and is therefore symbolic of the army. On the other, the picture promotes or suggests the idea that the French empire is large and benevolent, includes all sorts of people, extends its reach beyond the borders of France, and is like a large club that people of other nations aspire to belong to. Underneath the picture of a soldier is the myth-making venture of the French empire.

This is where writing comes into the picture. We want to be cognizant of the fact that we do not always mean what we say, we cannot always express ourselves, we sometimes try to say many things at once, we often substitute indirect speech for direct speech, we hang on to nuances and rely on tone, we use mood to alter the meaning of things, we manipulate vocabulary to try to broaden our statement, etc. No utterance is ever simple. No statement is only superficial or innocent. It is estimated that in communications, when we speak to another person, only ten percent of what we communicate is in the words themselves. The other 90 percent is transmitted by tone of voice, body language and gesture, pitch, speed, etc. What actually gets communicated in a speech act or a textual act is therefore uncertain. Paul Auster puts this more mysteriously in a discussion of the poet George Oppen, in an essay titled "Private I, Public Eye."[2] Auster describes Oppen's language as "almost naked," and he notes that Oppen's "syntax seems to derive its logic as much from the silences around words as from the words themselves" (115). The same, he claims, is true for the work of Giuseppe Ungaretti. "Ungaretti's poetic source," according to Auster, "is silence, and in one form or another, all his work is an expression of the inexhaustible difficulty of expression itself" (120).

Edmond Jabès makes similar claims for silence in writing in his interview with Auster. Jabès tells how close writing is to breathing and says that "what you might call the naked phrase—comes from a need to surround the words with whiteness in order to let them breathe" (154). Later Jabès remarks that "in this space between one word and the next," reading is possible. "Our reading takes place in the very whiteness between the words, for this whiteness reminds us of the much greater space in which the word evolves" (163). Jabès articulates the silent tension that exists between utterance and speechlessness. For him, the whole idea of "writer's block" is not so much a fear of losing the muse as it is a knowledge that the writer writes against silence. Jabès discusses how, after writing his poems, silence descends. "At those times you are filled with terrible doubt. You are afraid you

*Interesting* (N.B)

77

might never be able to write again. This is something extraordinary, something most people don't understand. Whenever you write you are running the risk of never writing again" (157). This bearing up against mortality is contrary to the idea of productivity that dominates our century, and it would be difficult to understand for those who do not write. Just the thought that, as Jabès says, the best books are the ones that destroy themselves so the writer has to start over all the time, indicates the precariousness of the uses and meanings of language (Auster, 164). Writing, like birdwatching, involves patience and silence. That writing poems should be like birdwatching is perhaps too mysterious a process to give it rational articulation. As Jabès says, "Writing comes in its own time...you can never force it" (157).

Paul Auster, whom one might see as a recent descendant of Blanchot, describes the same doubts in an essay on "The Death of Sir Walter Raleigh." Auster insists: "For we will never manage to say what we want to say, and whatever is said will be said in the knowledge of this failure" (75). Here we have the sad writer, speaking in the midst of a colossal, insurmountable silence. Yet there are ironies and contradictions to the problem of writing for Auster, as there are for Blanchot. Auster goes on to suggest that since we cannot say what we wish to say exactly, we nonetheless end up saying something, which is then construed further by the listener or reader. What we write ends up appearing in spite of the writer, somehow. In Auster's words, "thought nevertheless determines its own boundaries, and the man who thinks can now and then surpass himself, even when there is nowhere to go" (75). At the point of the impossibility of communication, meaning and evocation become possible again. "Where no possibility exists," he writes, "everything becomes possible again" (75).

The concerns about writing articulated by Auster, Jabès, Blanchot, Barthes, and others are about the larger field of semiotics. They are also about reception and performance. The writer's task is to know something about the hidden communications that bypass the writer's will to speak, or know about signals that escape from him. The writer has to be aware of the "hidden agendas" that surround us and, basically, to know the culture he is in. Then her task is to make that underground world of language, that mythological element in communication, apparent. To do this, any number of technical moves may be adopted: we can use excessive language; we can overwrite; we can fracture our discourse; we can speak in fragments; we can argue by analogy, etc. But no technical efficiency can make up for our lack of cultural, linguistic, semiotic awareness. Unless we understand the myths behind our discourses, we cannot learn how to unearth them, and whatever we may have learned about writing of a technical nature will not do us any good. Writing is here seen as an act on the edge of uncertainty. The writer touches the unknown in culture, in the self, and in language. All things are "pushed to the limit," to use Paul Auster's words. For Auster, "if language is to be pushed to the limit, then the writer must condemn himself to an exile of doubt, to a desert of uncertainty. What he must do, in effect, is create a poetics of absence" (114).

The idea that there could be something like a "poetics of absence" is not as mysterious as it may sound, nor as purposefully ironic. That there is an inherent mystery about the process of communicating through langue seems to be held in general agreement by writers everywhere. But the area of uncertainty that concerns them more is what happens in the vaster field of semiotics when we say or write something. This area of uncertainty is what Nigerian-born writer Ben Okri says is "beyond words."[3] In a brief essay he calls "Beyond Words," which is in his collection of such essays titled *A Way of Being Free,* Okri articulates some of what is meant by that uncertainty. He first echoes Italo Calvino in affirming that "our days are poisoned with too many words. Words said and not meant. Words said *and* meant. Words divorced from feeling. Wounding words. Words that conceal. Words that reduce. Dead words" (88). When words have lost their meaning, they are useless. They are, presumably, what Okri would classify as "bad words," as opposed to "good words." He rightly points out that "Good words enter you and become moods, become the quiet fabric of your being" (89). There is energy in words, which begins to occupy the reader. The writer's task is to make sure that energy is good energy. The wordless, which is the still part of the sentence, inspires the mood. Okri concludes, in the face of increased technology and its noise, that "we need more of the wordless in our lives. We need more stillness, more of a sense of wonder, a feeling for the mystery of life. We need more love, more silence, more deep listening, more deep giving" (90).

*NB.*

*Amen!*

Here I come to the anguish, one might say, of the unhappy teacher—the idea I began with. It is possible to teach others the technical aspects of writing. It is also possible to point out how to access some of our innermost thoughts. One may even convince another person how not to be afraid of the blank page and how to get over writer's block, and how to locate sources of inspiration. But if you do not intuit your people, your culture, the language you are using, the mythologies of our existence, and our continuous myth-making capacities, none of the things you are taught will be of use to you. If you are not able to function inside the uncertainties and doubts and absences the writing act will engage you in, you are lost before you begin. That insight into our mythologies, and into that condition of doubt required for writing, is not so teachable. Such a disposition is so deeply about you yourself: who you are, how you came to be that way, what your history is. The core of writing requires something that is very vulnerably personal, and yet at the same time very communal. That combination is what Blanchot calls mysterious. It is this core at the heart of writing that he would say is beyond the grasp of the average person—for whom our mythologies are not consequential enough, and for whom the world and its universe are more certain and safe than they are for the writer in the act of grasping the shifting nature of everything.

# 7 | On Writing Short Books

In his essay on the fiction of Jorge Luis Borges, which appeared in his book *A Writer's Reality*, Mario Vargas Llosa explains why it is that Borges writes short works. Borges, according to Vargas Llosa, despised the novel in its traditional form because it was so close to life, so mimetic, and therefore so imperfect. He wanted to transmute the clay of life into art. Vargas Llosa quotes Borges's foreword to *The Garden of Forking Paths*, where he writes that "the habit of writing long books, of extending to five hundred pages an idea that can be perfectly stated in a few months' time, is a laborious and exhausting extravagance" (Llosa, *Writer's* 11). Vargas Llosa does not agree with Borges, and cites *Moby Dick, Don Quixote, The Charterhouse of Parma*, as examples of the inadequacy of Borges's notion. However, he uses the quote to illustrate why Borges himself wrote the curt fiction he did.

A friend of mine who is a poet and who writes particularly terse poems, once expressed much the same sentiment. When asked why he didn't make his poems longer, he said "I don't want to waste anyone's time." That comment made more sense to me after perusing the essays of Italo Calvino. Calvino maintains that we are bombarded by an overuse, and therefore a cheapening, of language. The writer's task now, he maintains, is to cut down on the verbiage and get down to  clarity and the real beauty of a simple communicative act. The movement within modernism that we call minimalism is part of this line of thinking. Minimalists insist on the minimum use of words with which to say something. In this regard, William Carlos Williams's poem "The Red Wheelbarrow" is often cited. The complete text is: "so much depends/ upon/a red wheel/barrow/glazed with rain/water/beside the white/chickens." Many writers insist that it takes greater care and skill to write shorter works than longer ones. It was Sir Walter Scott who said, when asked why he wrote such long novels, that he didn't have time to make them shorter. Samuel Beckett provides us with another

*Notes to chapter 7 are on p. 113.*

example of a kind of minimalism that has philosophical purpose. For Beckett, as Paul Auster reminds us, "less is more" (89).

It is becoming a truism that there are too many words out there, and writers find the profusion of language intimidating. In a short essay called "Speaking of Writing: 'Spies with Music'," American writer Barry Hannah makes a point of wishing to do everything contrary to public expectation on account of the verbosity of modern times.[1] He wants to champion ignorance and be left alone by journalists and to read for things "incorrect," and write short books. He tells us plainly:

> I have gotten old enough to be a little bit humble about what is going on. One thing I have always realized is that I have written for an audience that knows as much as I do or more, and I am very conscious that there are too many words in the world. I work against the grain of the writer who is the conspicuous consumer of words. Like Ray Carver and some of the others attacked for "minimalism" now, I have always believed in compression and brevity. (207)

The assumption here is that short books, brief texts in book form, are somehow "incorrect" and go against the grain of the times. What is wanted and championed is the long book, the verbose tome, the panoramic performance, the epic and historical. Brevity is often considered weak—a sign of failure.

This view of brevity pops up in the fiction of A.S. Byatt. Byatt is known for exceedingly long works, in particular, her amazing novel _Possession_. This novel is so long that it has room for almost everything, in a Bakhtinian sense, and could be seen as truly postmodern. By contrast, in her later novel _The Biographer's Tale_, Byatt's narrator, Phineas G. Nanson, a graduate student in literature, has had enough of "postmodernism" and becomes hungry for "facts" and the "real" instead. He uses his graduate course as an example of something weak and tiresome: "We'd been doing a lot of not-too-long texts written by women. And also quite a lot of Freud" (1). He is tired of deconstructing everything and cannot, he admits, remember what they have been reading because "All the seminars, in fact, had a fatal family likeness. They were repetitive in the extreme" (1). But Byatt's Phineas is making the same apparent mistake as many others, by equating the short, especially the short and fragmentary book with deconstruction and postmodernism. This is not necessarily a leap one ought to make. There are many reasons for making a novel, if it is a novel, short rather than long, and some of those reasons are very good. It will also be seen that the idea of the short book as an art form practised mainly by women writers is far from true.

Edmond Jabès talks about brevity in writing as a form of fragmentation in his interview with Paul Auster. Jabès calls his book *The Book of Questions* a *récit éclaté*, a story in fragments. We cannot see the totality of things, he observes, and our vision is informed by the fragmentary nature of time itself. "Totality is an idea," he notes, "and it can be shown only through fragments" (Auster 162). The nature of a book is in itself fragmented; we read in fragments and conceive in bits and pieces. "We know that we are in something immense," he notes, "but at each moment we can only see what is in front of us… Totality is something we reconstitute for ourselves through all these fragments, because these fragments are what provides visibility" (162). As with the eye of the fly, we see in parcels, each part brief enough to absorb its idea. Only later, when all the fragments are put together, does the larger picture emerge.

On the same line of thought, Robert Kroetsch has written an interesting essay on the art or the idea of the scrapbook, titled "D-Day and After: Remembering a Scrapbook I Cannot Find," which appears in *A Likely Story.* Kroetsch tries to remember the most enduring images of the war years in Alberta and, after the painted legs of women who could not get hold of stockings but had to paint them on, the most lasting impression he has is of the scrapbook. As children in school were made to create scrapbooks, Kroetsch tells of how he laboured over his collage of newspaper articles and pictures and memorabilia. So much later in life he reminisces about what he was actually doing, which turns out to be much the same thing as what Edmond Jabès confesses he was doing when writing *The Book of Questions.* Kroetsch surmises that the people around him mainly wanted something intelligible to emerge from these scrapbooks. He claims that "They wanted someone to make an informing narrative of the confusion. They wanted someone to put the fragments—the scraps—into order" (134). For the makers of scrapbooks, however, the sense of participation emerged: "Scraps allowed us to participate in the story without being swallowed into invisibility" (135).

There is a conviction both for Kroetsch and Jabès that narrative, like real life, becomes perceptible in fragments. Not only is there a need to tell stories in small bits but there is an urge to make books that are, in themselves, only fragments of larger "books." Such very large books may never end, and perhaps the fragment, or the small story, the small book, is all there is. Kroetsch explains it this way:

*Big book, small story!*

> Yet the idea of scrap implies a larger whole, an organized universe, an explanatory mythology, from which the scrap was taken or has fallen away. Or it might harbour that implication.
>
> That doubt has informed a good deal of my notion of what writing is. What if the scraps are the story? Our lives on the prairies often went unrecorded; they survived as a collection of photographs in a shoe box, a scattering of stories told around a kitchen table. They survived as a scrapbook. (136)

Inside the fascination with scraps, Kroetsch also confesses, is the sense of living on the margin of "big" history. The "real" story is elsewhere, being fought on the fields of Europe, while those who wait at home are left with the "scraps," the leftovers of history. "Scraps are left over from the making of a book," he writes, "that is, from the making of a cohering narrative, from the establishment of beginning, middle, and end" (140-41). But paradoxically, there is no "real" narrative anywhere else, and the writer later recognizes that everyone feels like that, as if they are living only the leftovers of experience. There are, in other words, no "long, coherent books." Scraps and fragments can be books in themselves. Not only is the immediate environment experienced as the debris of something else, he implies, but in the speech act and the writing act, immediacy is experienced as a digression. The scrapbook for Kroetsch, therefore, also has in it "the notion of the interrupted story, or, more significantly, the digression" (146).

It is not necessary for many writers to have a philosophical reason for wishing to write short books. Writing is an exhausting, laborious, and draining exercise. To think of having to start a book that must be five hundred pages long is intimidating to the point of paralysis for the poetically inclined writer who pores over every word. For some, the idea of "overwriting" is simply unappealing. Tom Stoppard, for instance, once said in an interview on PBS that one of the reasons he was a playwright rather than a novelist was that plays are short. A play, he said, *A play, why not?* can be written in three months if you write a page a day. A scene of a four-act play need take no more than half an hour. Thinking in those terms makes playwriting suddenly "doable."

Robert Kroetsch approaches the idea of the novel as something that "can" be done when talking about Margaret Laurence's long novel *The Diviners* to illustrate something similar to what Stoppard is suggesting. The novel starts off with Morag the novelist going to her typewriter to write a long novel, only to find that her daughter Pique has run away from home and typed a goodbye note on the blank sheet of paper in the typewriter. Pique has written one paragraph. After receiving this paragraph, Morag writes a long novel responding to her daughter's departure. To Kroetsch, however, it is Pique's paragraph that is the real novel. Morag, instead, is really writing a long footnote, which could, as footnotes go, be without end (Kroetsch 148-56). Everything the mother goes on to say has already been implied in the daughter's one-paragraph "novel."

In an essay on the writing of poetry, Anne Michaels, who writes both poetry and award-winning novels, talks about the necessity and inevitability of the kind of fragmenting of experience spoken of by Jabès and Kroetsch.[2] In "Cleopatra's Love," Michaels makes the observation that the poem is, by nature, a short text because it needs to render "as many layers of experience as possible" in every line. To make such a rich, multivalent, layered text "long" would be exhausting. A poem has to remain "unified without loss of complexity" (179). More than the complexity and layeredness of a poem, however, a poem "knows" that there is no coherence or unity. Everything, it is implied by poetry itself, is partial. Michaels writes that "with luck, [the poem] manages to capture an instant partially, suggestive of the whole" (179). Such a suggestiveness is the best a text can do, she goes on to say, because "our knowledge is always partial…we never learn the whole story but assume instead that truth lies somewhere hidden among these perceptions" (179). Given that we cannot know "the whole story," it would be absurd to try to master an entire narrative in all its parts and provide closure to it as well. The short book, the short story, and the shorter poem, can all be suggestive of a larger whole which, the poet knows, cannot really be rendered anyway.

What these comments on the short book by various writers suggests is that the short book, regardless of its overt "genre," tends toward the fragmented, the poetic, and the theoretical. The brevity of the work, if it is not more than a hundred and fifty pages, for example, creates a pressure on its author to make each page worthwhile. The silence itself, which occurs between fragments, needs to become eloquent. For many, it is the eloquence of everything, from the sentences to the margins to the spaces between paragraphs, that constitutes the challenge and the appeal of the short book. The short book has in common with poetry that it can be read more than once and, in fact, is meant to be read again. Unlike the very long novel, which can be very long only if each word is not too intense, the short book does not need to be "consumed" as a consumer item.[3] So the shelf life of the short book ought to be much longer. When publishers and bookstores and distributors treat the brief, intensely written narrative as if it were a novel, they are depriving the short book of its essential benefit. It is difficult, for example, to think of Elizabeth Smart's *By Grand Central Station I Sat down and Wept*, which is an example of the brief, intensely written, poetic narrative I am talking about here, as having any kind of "shelf life" in a market economy. Such a book has to be lived with rather than simply read and put aside for the next one.

Examples of the kind of short book I am talking about abound. One curious thing, however, is that the intense, brief, intergeneric narrative (if one can call it that) is practised more widely, and more conspicuously and with better results, outside of North America than in. I became interested in the short book long ago after reading Françoise Sagan, Margurerite Duras, and Colette, French women writers; Tove Ditlevsen, a Danish writer; and Anaïs Nin, an American in France. Another, later, discovery of this type of book was Clarise Lispector's *The Stream of Life*.[4] Of well-known and current works that belong in the same category, we can point to Albert Camus's *The Outsider*, as an example of brevity, intensity, philosophical depth, and poetic style. This narrative is a fascinating exploration of justice. The protagonist ends up committing a crime, namely, murdering a man on the beach, without exactly intending to. The murder could be seen as self-defence, and it could be seen as a manifestation of an illness he is not articulating. The symptoms of his illness are a great sensitivity to light, a peculiar fatigue and vertigo, an inability to register the importance of things (or an inability to feel). He has not slept or eaten well, and has been drinking in the heat, so on top of it all he is probably dehydrated. He says himself that "by nature my physical needs often distorted my feelings" (65).

The trial that follows is painfully unjust and the facts are distorted. But the prisoner is not especially affected by what is happening to him, nor that he will perhaps end up being put to death. He discovers along the way the existential realities that characterize Camus's thought. He says at one point about being in prison, when comparing it to freedom, that "you ended up getting used to everything" (75). Similarly, he discovers, when ostensibly speaking of the trial, that "Everything is true and yet nothing is true" (88). All is, in fact, chance. Everything is an accident. His life wisdom after all this is the realization that "a familiar journey under a summer sky could as easily end in prison as in innocent sleep" (94). Nothing really matters. Justice does not exist either, because "the qualities of an ordinary man could be used as damning evidence of guilt" (97). just as easily as of innocence. The whole object of the exercise of writing the book, and of telling this story, is that there is nothing much one can say. So there is no reason to take a long time saying it. For Camus, therefore, brevity of narration is in itself a philosophical position.[5]

A sort of "descendant" of Camus, insofar as he writes of the same geography and the same climate, and shows some of the same "symptoms" as Camus, is Moroccan writer Abdelkebir Khatibi.[6] Khatibi is also an academic, and his writing is infused with philosophical and theoretical problems and discourses. The book that is here a good example of the brief, intense narrative as it is practised at its most extreme, is his novelistic essay on bilingualism, *Love in Two Languages*. The story concerns a North African Arab man and a French woman who have a love affair that is infused with all the problems of interculturalism, bilingualism, and long distance. In other words, this is a "mixed marriage," and Khatibi contemplates in a peculiarly hystericized way most of the problems an intercultural relationship like that has to offer.

What is evident for the reader is, first, that the narrator has so much to say that, paradoxically, it seems futile to say any of it. The "essay," if one could call this novel that, is packed with emotions, thoughts, speculations, observations, sensations, and is completely self-contradictory. That is also its point: such a love relationship is anything but unified and developmental. A regular novel of more than two hundred pages would suffer from the chaos of this type of story, told honestly and fearlessly. At one point the narrator exclaims, in fact, something that is reminiscent of Camus: that "he had a premonition that this disturbance [within himself] had caused him to gradually imagine everything, to invent it all out of his own obsessions" (14). In other words, he begins to doubt his sense of reality, and perception itself is questioned. Like the narrator of *The Outsider*, Khatibi's protagonist suffers from fatigue, vertigo, blurred vision, and a sense of unreality. This may be due to the heat and light specific to North Africa, but the sense that everything matters and nothing matters simultaneously is evident in both books.

Khatibi, like Camus, has a vision of a "great freedom in distress" (27) which characterizes the tone of the whole narrative. The narrator says of himself, which is also by extension about the narrative he is producing, that "he had made no progress in any direction. Thrashing around in one place, he had the impression that he was going to be done away with" (34). He also realizes, like Camus's prisoner, that everything is very much like nothing. The more you say, the less gets said. He asserts that "I write what I don't say to your face: writing spares me any kind of revelation. Read, read some more, you'll never read enough" (35). At such a juncture, it becomes apparent that there is no point in making this book longer. There is enough of an experience packed into the book already to make it possible to be read many times, and be a different book each time. The great metaphor in *Love in Two Languages* is the sea, which is an image for language itself. The narrator dives into it many times and is carried by the current to the unknown. Also like Camus, Khatibi exclaims through the narrator the underlying philosophy of futility and injustice: "Guilty of nothing, under what law was I being convoked?" (95). Regardless of what he does, in other words, he will suffer, because life itself is like that. In an epilogue, in fact, Khatibi writes of how his readers are mystified by the "genre" of his narrative. He says, "If I were asked, Is your story a new *nouveau roman*? Or, better, a bi-novel new novel? I'd reply that the novel never had any affection for me. We don't have the same history" (115). Nevertheless, it seems that his book is marketed as if it were the novel it claims not to be.

As Khatibi's narrator points out, one of the principal characteristics of the short "novel" is that its genre is often in question. There is a difference between the novella and the short novel, and there is a difference between the latter and what might be seen as an extended short story. But the intention here is not to dive into genre studies, but rather to place the short narrative that stands on its own as a book into the foreground and see some of its inevitable angles. J.M. Coetzee's short novel *Foe* is a good example of what kind of mix-up such a work can look like even when it appears to be just a regular novel. The narrative is told from the point of view of a Susan Barton, who has been shipwrecked and ended up on Crusoe's island, where she befriends both him and Friday. But Crusoe dies and Barton and Friday are rescued, and end up in England looking for Foe. The protagonist's idea is to find the writer of *Robinson Crusoe* so he can write her story before it has been written. She will be his muse and he will be the writer. Much of this "novel" is a discourse on writing instead of a "story," and the real interest of the narrative is the discussion it proposes on writing and its inspirations. As a "regular" novel this book might be seen as a failure, but as a somewhat fictionalized discussion on writing, it is interesting.

Yet another example we can take for this literary phenomenon is Susanna Tamaro's novel *Follow Your Heart*.[7] Tamaro is Italian, and this book has been popular in Europe, perhaps because the type of book it is has more of a precedent there than in North America. *Follow Your Heart* is composed as a series of letters a grandmother writes to her granddaughter. The driving impulse for writing them is that the granddaughter has rebelled and left home, and the relationship with her family is not good. The grandmother sets out to clear the air and finally tell the truth about her own life, which for better or worse will set the record straight. She knows if she does not say these things, the tension and rift between herself and her granddaughter will remain, and nothing will be gained. So she takes the risk, and the narrative accumulates around her in a flock of letters she does not send, but knows will be found after her death.

What characterizes Tamaro's brief novel is not the story, which only slowly crystallizes for the patient reader, but the opportunity this format allows the narrator to be reflective. Every letter proceeds the way epistles usually do: there is a little information and a lot of reflection around it. We get to know the letter writer rather well; how she feels and what she thinks about small things like the flowers in her garden or the pet dog she has, or the life she has shared with her family. In the hands of a more rigid philosopher, a book like this could be highly educational, and precedents abound in the world of literature for philosophy expounded in the form of letters to individuals. But Tamaro is not as much of a philosopher as she is reflective and a humanist, and there is no pressure on the reader to have any background except that of breathing, in order to appreciate the various truths of what her narrator is saying.

The book is brief for reasons other books are brief. The narrator knows on some level her efforts at explaining herself are futile. She says at one point the world is too noisy, and going too fast, for understanding to take place at all. "Understanding demands silence," she writes. You cannot say too much, for then you will not be heard. "Words imprison the mind," she writes (92). She is trying to create a small opening wherin she can point her granddaughter in a direction that will make her wiser. But the truths that emerge are similar to the truths of Camus and Khatibi. At the bottom, there is nothing, except what you are able to make of things yourself. She advises her reader:

> The only master that exists, the only one that's true and believable is your own conscience. To find it you have to stand in silence—alone and in silence—you have to stand on the naked earth, naked your-

> self and with nothing around you, as if you were already dead. You
> don't hear anything at first, the only thing you feel is terror. (178)

The value of silence and the experience of emptiness are central, it appears, to the nature of the brief narrative that is intense, poetic, reflective if not philosophical, and still tells a story.

Finally, there is one type of narrative that seems made for this "short novel" genre discussed here, and that is the adult "fairy tale." We sometimes link the idea of the fairy tale that might be enjoyed by adults to something like Tolkien's *The Lord of the Rings*. Tolkien's work is long and complex, and what reflective wisdom it has to offer is not as obvious as Alessandro Baricco's very short novel *Silk*.[8] Perhaps this is the most pointed example of the "genre" of the short novel because it is truly short and narrated in very brief fragments. Some fragments are only half a paragraph, and the rest of the page is allowed to stay empty. The result is similar to what we get with poetry: the empty space becomes a large part of the narrative itself. We are asked to use it, and we get a chance to think about what we have read. The book is a "fairy tale" because it tells an unlikely story that is close enough to life as we know it to make us wish to suspend our imagination.

The story is about Hervé Joncour, a French silkworm merchant who, in 1861, when travel was not that common, repeatedly goes to Japan to get larvae for the French silk industry. He has to travel beyond the known world, in French terms, and the story has the characteristics of a dream as well as a fable. Baricco skips the details of the journey, and dwells only on the more hypnotic and spellbinding aspects of the experience, which are amplified by the massive silences between chapters. The journey, as well as the silk worms themselves, become symbolic and of philosophical import. The relationship between life and desire itself is also amplified, because inside the journey there is an erotic attraction that compels Joncour to continue doing what he does. The idea seems to be that we are driven in life by impulses not of our own making. Something grips us which is larger than us, and we need to follow its course. If we do not, we have not existed. This is the "lesson" that is also articulated by Susanna Tamaro, and the short book that is full of space and ambiguity is therefore ideal for the intimate knowledge this idea encapsulates. If to follow one's fate, to let go and allow the "sea" of fate to take over, to refer to Khatibi's image, is an idea one ought not to take up before harsh philosophical scrutiny, this is the kind of "secret wisdom" that is ideally represented in a fairy tale.

A very famous short book in America is Anne Morrow Lindbergh's *Gift from the Sea,* first published in 1955, and continually reprinted since. This is a meditation, written in the most serious and honest manner, by a woman who has taken a break from a busy family life to vacation by the sea alone, in a small shack with few amenities. She organizes her meditation around the idea of randomly scattered sea shells she finds on her walks at the beach. Each chapter is an elaboration of the metaphor of the particular shell she is contemplating (channelled whelk, moon shell, double-sunrise, oyster bed, argonauta). Using the shells as signposts to her thoughts, she contemplates solitude, modern life, women's lives, and relationships. Her thesis is that we should all find time to be alone and let our minds drift naturally, like the sea and its shells We become wiser in doing so, and realize that our ambitions, greeds, fears, and anxieties are things we can let go of. We also realize, as she has, that no relationships (marriage and even children) are entirely enduring, and in the end we are simply alone. She does not need to spill a lot of words to write this message; instead the book is as modest as what it has to say. What it says is: let go. The eight chapters in *Gift from the Sea* seem to be just as randomly given to the author as a collection of stones or shells would be if accidentally found on a beach walk. "The beach is not the place to work; to read, write or think" (15) she begins her book by saying. The book itself is like the beach. The small recitation is in itself not a place of imaginative or intellectual scrutiny, but a book for a reader to lose herself in.

Another obvious adult "fairy tale" is Brazilian writer Paulo Coelho's *The Alchemist.*[9] This novel is so far into its fairy-tale genre that it is hardly even read as fiction, but rather as life wisdom and modern humanism set out in the form of a fable. In this story, an Andalusian shepherd named Santiago ends up following the advice of strangers and paying attention to omens along the way in his quest for what he calls his "personal legend." The "lesson" is the same as in Tamaro, which is to "follow your heart," and this is a poetic idea that needs poetic expression. The reason *The Alchemist* is so popular is that it offers a kind of "hope" people generally wish for. Early on in the tale, a man tells the shepherd: "people are capable, at any time in their lives, of doing what they dream of" (24). The objective of the boy's quest is to discover how that statement is actually true and how one goes about it. The answer is, you let go, you allow fate to take over, and you pay attention to signs and synchronicities. At bottom, all of this is a mystery, and therefore the ambiguity of the telling, the leaps in logic, the absence of detail and the flavour of the dream, all conspire to reinforce the sense of awe that is required for any of our dreams to actually come true, the narrative suggests. As another old man advises the shepherd, "when you really want something, the universe always conspires in your favor" (38). Such a world view is completely antithetical to what we have heard from Camus, Khatibi, Cain, Smart, and other short-novel writers like Kate Chopin in *The Awakening*. But we are dealing with a difference in the short-novel genre when looking at Coelho and Tamaro and Baricco.

Coelho's Santiago discovers that "books are like caravans" the way camels are in the desert and the way wisdom is transferred from individual to individual. That books are dependent on each other becomes abundantly clear when observing the short book. They rely on each other extensively, mention each other, and are often very intertextual in nature. This reliance on intertexts takes us back to Edmond Jabès: each book is only a fragment of the great library of humanity, just as Lindbergh might say that each book thrown up to us is just a piece in the vast multitude of treasures harboured by the sea (by language itself). But more than that, as Abdelkebir Khatibi shows, you can read one and then another and another book, but you will never have read enough. Because at bottom, we cannot really say what we need to express: that is the import of the short book. The truth is always beyond us, and instead of packing our lives with words, we can draw back and say much less, but make each word count more, and fill each word with the mystery and awe language deserves. Therefore the short book, even the fragmentarily written book, the poetic narrative that resembles a fairy tale or a fable, the philosophical treatise, and the *récit*, are all able to come together in what seems to be a format that suits the intergeneric nature of short books. For the poetic writer, this format can be ideal.

# 8 | Poetry and the Idea of Home

The idea of "home" is complex and fluctuates depending on the discipline from which it is examined. Within poetry and poetic theory, however, there is an interesting line of thought that uses the language and conceptualization of "home" that is particular to poetry. Poets have their own associations, theories, imagerial constructs, and emotional expressions that seem to be unique to poetry. The whole idea that there could be a "home" at all, a place of safety and comfort, is in many ways the essential compass point of poetry itself. There is a poem by Wislawa Szymborska, a Polish poet who won the Nobel Prize for Literature in 1996, which is simply called "Going Home," and which can be cited to illustrate one of the ways in which poetry may think of itself as home.[1] In this poem, a grown man comes home after a day's work as an academic scientist who lectures on "homeostasis in megagalactic cosmonautics" and lies down on his bed, curled up in a fetal position with the blanket pulled over his head. The implication is that something is dreadfully wrong and this man's response is to return to a womb-like condition for security, "in sheltered darkness." Here, Szymborska speaks of the idea of home, as well as home itself, the way it would occur to a poet. In this poem, "home" is not so much a place, even though the person she speaks of is in fact going to his house and his bedroom. Rather, home is a primeval memory, an attitude of forgetting, a physical posture. Szymborska is talking about consciousness in the world. "Something has gone wrong" for the persona of the poem, which could be anything, important or not, and he needs a refuge from the world. The refuge is sleep, but it is also quiet; it is the private chamber, the blanket, the darkness. Most interestingly, the protagonist is sheltered by a moment of eternity which is also a memory of the womb. Here is the locus of the poem itself, writing about itself.

The house, the bed, sleep, the womb: all these are attributes of poetic "home" in Szymborska's poem. Something has gone wrong on the out-

*Notes to chapter 8 are on p. 114.*

side of these enclosures. This outside has been referred to by Don McKay, one of Canada's most notable poets, as "wilderness." What the poet seeks shelter from could be an ambiguous thing, and what constitutes the shelter itself is also uncertain. But the dichotomy between "home" and "wilderness" is of some interest north of the forty-ninth parallel, and the concept of wilderness is used to describe the outer world where things go wrong by Canadian poets because there is a lot of wilderness in Canada. In an essay titled "Baler Twine: Thoughts on Ravens, Home, and Nature Poetry," included in Tim Lilburn's collection *Poetry and Knowing,* Don McKay talks about the ways in which both concepts are constructed for the writer. McKay posits that both home and wilderness are equally central to the poetic mind, but one (home) is a state of possessing, grasping appropriation, and the other (wilderness) is a state of letting go. The persona in Szymborska's poem, by extension, is perhaps "grasping" or "possessing" the posture that constitutes safety, out of the surrounding chaos. McKay explains, on the other hand, that by "wilderness" he means "not just a set of endangered spaces, but the capacity of all things to elude the mind's appropriations" (21). Wilderness, or chaos, can be anything that you either do not own or control or even desire. "To what *degree* do we own our houses, hammers, dogs?" McKay asks. "Beyond that line lies wilderness" (21).

Many poets argue that to be a writer at all, you need to remain open to chaos, or wilderness. You should be prepared to take the prototypical nature journey of Henry David Thoreau, or the spiritual journey of Thomas Merton, and just let go. That is where writing begins. However, that wilderness, that unknown chaos into which the writer journeys, needs to be countered by its opposite: the idea of home, to which the poet is equally drawn, out of an equal necessity. Here is where possession occurs. McKay explains the contrast of "home" as "the action of the inner life finding out form; it is the settling of self into the world" (21). The peacefulness that comes with the assurance of control, he implies, is also a prerequisite for writing. It is a state in which the writer can "settle" the world. Here the metaphor of settling land and its connection to writing is made explicit. It is why settlers write. Home is a place, but also a state of mind, as is wilderness. Don McKay thinks of home as important "because it substantiates the self (even a name, John Berger points out, is a home in a minimal sense) and separates it from the world. It establishes a *place* where representation and recollection occur, and breaks the plenum of experience" (22). When Wordsworth thought of poems as "recollections in tranquility," he might have been in conversation with McKay here. Because it is wilderness that is being recollected, but the tranquility required for it is home. A certain "double axis" is therefore formed by the notion of home and wilderness being equally important for the poet to write, and the poem to appear.

The idea of home as refuge from a world where things go drastically wrong, and this refuge including sleep and memories of the womb, as we see in Szymborska's poem, is taken further in a poem called "Jihad Sounds of Home" by German poet and novelist Marcel Beyer.[2] This poem appeared in the journal *Poetry* in 1998, in a translation by Margitt Lehbert. The speaker here is at home, but cannot rest because he has neighbours from some part of the world where there is war and anger, and this international war cry enters his world through a cassette recording playing outside. The speaker hears the cassette playing in the courtyard below. It is dark and, though they are in Germany, the music is Egyptian. He reminisces about childhood things like cookies and sofas and "unmade beds," about "blue-film dummies," "soap flakes," and snow. Such images freely associate while the "wild" music carries into his daydreams. These young men "down in the courtyard" are from elsewhere and their foreign music, with their cousin singing along in "his rough voice," interrupts the peaceful atmosphere of the narrator's memories. The sounds of reality are of a child crying and of cars on the street. Something is terribly disturbed in the speaker's home, and a new unfamiliarity has broken in. The sound that disturbs him is the human cry: the music that sounds like jihad to him and the crying of the child in the morning are indications that he can never escape the human condition, the sufferings of others, because they are also his own. He is awakened while still at home to the reality that "wilderness" in this case is war and has made itself felt. He has recollections of war he has not experienced, of wilderness he has not been in himself. He is learning how to make himself at home in the "jihad sounds."

As we recollect, therefore, we also possess. We even appropriate when we remember. The theory and science of memory is very complex and has to be discussed elsewhere, but the site for memory may still be constituted as a kind of home.[3] In McKay's words, "home is also the site of our appreciation of the material world, where we lavish attention on its details, where we collaborate with it" (22). In fact, when the poet "lavishes attention" on the details of an environment, there is a kind of creation-of-home occurring. Deborah Keahey, who is one of the only Canadian theorists who has written extensively on the notion of home creation in Canadian literature, speaks of this act in writing as "home-making." The poem itself, therefore, becomes the site for that attention. The poem is, in itself, home. Don McKay has another way of saying just this about language, poem, and home. He notes that "we might try to sum up the paradox of home-making [poem-writing] by saying that inner life *takes place*: it both *claims* place and acts to become a place among others. It turns wilderness into interior and presents interiority to the wilderness" (22). Here McKay is actually speaking of a state of mind as a place in itself, which, when written (about), becomes home.

A poem by Marina Tsvetaeva, who was born in Moscow but lived much of her life in Prague, illustrates on some level McKay's notion of the poem itself being the only possible construct of "home" for a poet.[4] Here Tsvetaeva also expands the idea of home to the social and political sphere. For her, the poem is "home" because nothing else qualifies. There is no other home possible when you live in exile. She comes to the search for home by eliminating all that home is not, which includes all the conventional formulations of the idea of home. Her poem "Homesickness," from *The Ratcatcher*, is an example of how the poem turns in on itself to illustrate that it is, itself, what all the other things it mentions fail to be. Here the narrator is ranting, more or less, in cynical anger over the idea of being nostalgic and homesick. She no longer cares about "home" because her condition of unhappiness is the same wherever she is: "It's all the same to me now / where I am altogether lonely." She is equally lonely, equally a misfit and equally misunderstood, whether she is at home in Russia or in exile somewhere else. She scoffs at the whole idea that you can feel at home anywhere. But then she sees a rowanberry bush by the side of the road, and despite herself she has a moment of being transported. She does not tell us by what, or to what, but presumably she is transported by some sort of memory, by a personal sense of home. Home is not society, not culture, not language, not even literature. Instead, she ends her poem with a dreamy reach towards a sight and a smell, the memory of which has lingered in her mind since some forgotten time. That moment of transcendence becomes home, and is "placed" into the poem, which is the only place where it can exist.

The rowanberry for Tsvetaeva is a wilderness point in this poem that intersects with the poet's life and sense of self, to use Don McKay's analogy. Nothing else in life has served; not even the age-old standby, "nativity" or ethnicity. But the sense of smell can, and does, create an impression of home which is in fact poetic, and which gives rise to writing. She needs the incursion of wilderness to get directions "home" again, and this is what the rowanberry does in her poem. Deborah Kehey, in her study on "home-making" in prairie literature, mentions Wallace Stegner in the same context as an example of the reality of this incursion of wilderness, and the gravity of what Tsvetaeva is saying in "Homesickness." Stegner is from Whitemud, Saskatchewan, but has spent his life away from there. Although he thinks of the area around Whitemud as "home," it is not the town or people he is talking about, any more than it is place or people for Tsvetaeva. Keahey quotes Stegner, who insists that the sense of home for him is the

> "tantalizing and ambiguous and wholly native smell" of the shrub wolf willow. Smelling this plant's leaves again after "forty alien years" collapses time and erases history, so that "the queer adult compulsion to return to one's beginnings" is assuaged. A contact has been made, a mystery touched. For the moment, reality is made exactly equivalent with memory, and a hunger is satisfied. (Keahey 5)

There is an architectural model for the kind of intersection of wilderness and home which Marina Tsvetaeva and Wallace Stegner refer to. Home for these poets is not the conventional thing people think it is. Home is a "mystery" that exists inside the poet's sense of longing. Don McKay points to John Berger to elucidate and substantiate what he is saying, and Berger's spatialization of what is essentially a very personal mystery. He introduces Berger's argument with a note on humanism when he says:

> Inside humanistic thinking, it is often useful to construe home as a crossing place, an intersection of Axes. John Berger, developing an idea of Mircea Eliade's, sees home as a place where, at least until our century, the world could be founded and made sense of, the heart of the real. (22)

McKay quotes the following passage from John Berger, where Berger architecturalizes this whole intersection. Berger writes that

> Home was the center of the world because it was the place where a vertical line crossed with a horizontal one. The vertical line was a path leading upwards to the sky and downwards to the underworld. The horizontal line represented the traffic of the world, all the possible roads leading across the earth to other places. Thus, at

home, one was nearest to the gods in the sky and to the dead in the underworld. This nearness promised access to both. And at the same time, one was at the starting point and, hopefully, the returning point of all terrestrial journeys. (McKay 23)

The poetic innuendoes in this image are worth noting. The horizontal line is, perhaps, wilderness. The vertical line is transcendence. The intersection is, significantly enough, home itself. It is hard not to think of the theorizing that has appeared concerning prairie literature with this imagery in mind: the idea of "horizontal world, vertical man."[5]

The sense of home as the place where vertical and horizontal axes cross may be present in the poem itself. The horizontal line of a railway track or a highway may cross with the vertical line of the man standing up (or the telephone pole where communication takes place, or the house, where habitation and society take place), where depth and width meet. Dennis Lee, who is a well-known Canadian poet, proposes this merging of home-as-poem; as longing; as direction and intention; and as the axis of two lines crossing in a poem which appeared back in 1974 in the journal *boundary 2*, and is titled "400: Coming Home." In this poem, the narrator is standing by the side of the road. We do not know why he is there, but he is watching the cars speed by and behind him is the "scrub-grass, the fences, / the fields." It appears that "back in the city" he has escaped from, his world has somehow collapsed; "many things you lived for/ are coming apart," he tells himself. He thinks of young people in the city listening to rock music and then listens to the cicadas in the night. He is eerily alone at some crossroads we know nothing of except its existential import. The narrator is either hitch-hiking or waiting or just standing on the road, and he is attentive to the grasses, fences, the crows, cars, and he notes the absence of houses in the scene. Something is amiss. We do not know why he is there or where he is going, but the home he is alluding to is, as he says, "coming apart" and has disintegrated. He is in wilderness (he "inhabits it"), and has to make do with that.

When McKay is talking about wilderness as a state of mind, he means a kind of "poetic attention" which is bestowed on a scene (24). Qualifying this state, he explains that "it's a sort of readiness, a species of longing which is without the desire to possess, and it does not really wish to be talked about" (24). That mentality is different from the state of mind which is "home." The poem itself, often made to stand for the whole idea of "home" in poetic commentaries, is an engagement with wilderness in such a way that a connection is made and a kind of metaphorical "settling" of the human spirit has taken place inside chaos. McKay notes that "to me, this is a form of knowing which counters the 'primordial grasp' in home-making, and celebrates the wilderness of the other; it gives ontological applause" (24). On the one hand, therefore, we give "ontological applause" in wilderness, and we write it out in the form of a "settling" of the self, which constitutes home.

Tim Lilburn, a noted Saskatchewan poet, engages in a similar discussion in his essay "How to Be Here?" which appeared in the same book. Lilburn frames his discussion differently, and without the binaries McKay imposes on our thinking about "home" versus "wilderness." Lilburn speaks instead of poetry in a more intense, even ecstatic way, and wishes to let the poetic sensibility go into the state of "wilderness" rather than be constrained by "home." To Lilburn, paradoxically, wilderness is, in fact, home. Home for the poet is the acceptance of the fact that union with the world cannot be achieved. There is always loss, always grief at separation. Lilburn writes that "when consciousness crosses the divide into the wilderness of what is there, it expects to find a point of noetic privilege: at last a clear view into the heart of things. But what it does find on the other side is further peculiarity, a new version of distance" (162). The concept of difference is central to the poet's understanding of where she can be at home. "The world is a collection of oddnesses, things so gathered into themselves," Lilburn writes, "so ruthlessly at home and separate, they seem to shine with difference" (162).

At the heart of poetic consciousness, Lilburn's argument attests, is the idea of mourning. Mourning and poetry fuse because in the poem's homesickness, home is never achieved. This is not a matter of actual distance or geography, but rather one of consciousness, for "one does miss the homeland of being where one is" (175). It is a matter of attention. He writes that "poetry in its incompleteness awakens a mourning over the easy union with the world that seems lost" (172). The poet wishes to praise the world, but "beyond praise is lament; the fact of the thing is still far away" (172). Home as a sensibility, a concept, a poetic attitude, is here aligned with the mystical and the tragic, and is caught up in the very idea of longing. This notion alludes back to Marina Tsvetaeva's poem "Homesickness," where the thought of the rowanberry elicits the sense of home in the poem. It is the longing for the place that matters, not the possession of it. And as Lilburn attests, you can long for the place you are in; you can be homesick for the very place in which you reside.

The fusion of the act of poetry, the poetic "attention" Lilburn talks about, with mourning and a distance that produces longing, is carried out in a peculiarly stark way in a poem by Olga Broumas, a noted American poet.[6] I am thinking of a poem she titles "Landscape with Poets," which appeared in *Soie Sauvage*. Broumas's poems are invariably complex and dense, but in this poem she talks simply about her fellow poet John Berryman, who "jumped off a bridge," perhaps to his death.[7] The speaker, presumably also a poet, is standing on a bridge on the Willamette River, recalling Berryman's leap, and how the poet waved his arm, threw himself from the bridge, broke the ice of the river, and drifted downstream. Eventually the poet merges with the breaking ice floes, with killer whales, and finally with the "heart" itself. Broumas equates the poet, both on the bridge and the poet who has jumped off, with something primeval that has to fuse with the land, but is nonetheless fluid and uncertain. What she thinks of is full of mystery, but the place she is standing in is the axis of wilderness and civilization, of the cosmos and home. This axis has nothing to do with conventional ideas of how we settle on the earth as a species. The presence of the poet is something that is mourned and lost, but is also (in) the poem itself. We see that into the arena of "home," which is also a code word for "safety" and "security," enters its opposite: namely, tragedy, uncertainty, mourning, loss, chaos, violence, and death. Where we had loss in Dennis Lee's poem, we have violent death in Olga Broumas's poem, and intimations of war and anger hover in Marcel Beyer's poem.

Loss and death as part and parcel of the poet's sense of home is an equation presented starkly in a poem by Polish poet Zbigniew Herbert, and worth nothing here.[8] The poem is called "Home" and was published in the *Kenyon Review* in 1999, in the translation of John and Bogdana Carpenter. The speaker is allowing the image of home to come apart right in the poem itself, and we see the disintegration as if it were a pulverizing film:

A home above the year's seasons
home of children animals and apples
a square of empty space under an absent star

home was the telescope of childhood
the skin of emotion
a sister's cheek
branch of a tree

the cheek was extinguished by flame
the branch crossed out by a shell
over the powdery ash of the next
a song of homeless infantry

home is the die of emotion
home is the cube of childhood

the wing of a burned sister

leaf of a dead tree (19, with translator's permission)

It is the narrator-poet who holds these images together, and in himself maintains the idea of home, although home is burned and shelled.

To return to Tim Lilburn for a moment, whose argument is that the question of "home" and "wilderness" is really a question about self and other. The poet needs to merge, in some sense, with the "other," but is always incapable of completing the task. The longing for empathy cannot be assuaged. According to Lilburn, "the desire to feel otherness as selfhood never goes away" (162). The desire to do so is embedded in language itself, as Jacques Lacan might tell us. Therefore there is grief. Lilburn uses the image of two startled deer and the poet encountering each other, both sides staring, unable to really recognize each other. The man and the deer are essentially separate. Yet the poet feels an urge to involve himself in the Keatsian "negative capability" that would give him solace. The poet's task is therefore very much like the contemplative's mission, and as the essay proceeds, Lilburn interchanges the term *poet* and *contemplative* indiscriminately. It is not that naming things will close the distance between self and other, he argues. The contemplative knows that simply naming is not really knowing, and if you think you do "know," your knowledge of the world is "without courtesy" (163). For Lilburn, "the desire to belong to what the deer belongs to, the wildness, the thereness, is mortified but remains true" (163).

The wish to merge self and other, to make wilderness home, is fraught with the idea of nostalgia. The impulse to write poetry is a nostalgic impulse, which Lilburn also emphasizes. Desire, which is so central to writing, has in it an element of nostalgia. Both Szymbroska and Tsvetaeva have illustrated this reality in their poems, and what they show is a very primitive, primeval, and biological nostalgia at work. Inevitably, such a nostalgia is an impulse towards a longing for what cannot be acquired or achieved. A longing for a lost childhood, a lost Atlantis in myth, and the lost Paradise in religious thought. But those tropes (childhood, Atlantis, Paradise) are actually embellishments of an idea of "home" which only poetry can hone in on. Lilburn explains that "poetry's audacity, its appetite for embellishment, makes it elastic in its accommodations of awe, makes it home to a sweep of the most extravagant human desires. More than any other speech, poetry is tolerant of a nostalgia for Paradise" (163). That kind of "nostalgia" is what Lilburn, in line with theorizations of desire in language (e.g., Butler, Kristeva, Derrida, Barthes) calls desire, and "poetry is the artifact of that desire" (163). Lilburn further embellishes this thought, and poetically explains that "poetry is consciousness dreaming of domicile at the core of the foreign world, the mind deeply homesick and scheming return." Also, poetry is "mind remembering the old world of the Garden," where life is "adorned with the plumage of awareness" (164). To be home is, therefore, to be in the poem and fully alive in language.

For both of these Canadian poets therefore, McKay and Lilburn, the concept of home is not a question of place so much as it is a factor of language (McKay) and contemplation itself (Lilburn). These two writers are in alliance with what Deborah Keahey has found in Canadian prairie writing in a more general sense. In her book-length study *Making It Home*, Keahey points out that many prairie writers equate home with things like culture or community more than with place itself, and for these writers it is not necessarily true that "home is singular and locatable—pinpointable—in space" (3). In talking about the poetry of several Saskatchewan poets, Keahey notes that home is "created" in the sense that it is "space inscribed by cultural, psychological, and social significance" (4). In more general terms therefore, "place and the home place are not absolute givens but are flexible constructions" (4). Referring to the poetry of Robert Kroetsch, she recognizes "the way the poems *themselves* construct space and home." This effect, which is what Don McKay has elaborated on in his essay, is what Keahey calls "literary homemaking" (4). This idea stands in a kind of opposition to "realist" and "deterministic" notions in studies of Canadian literature—notions that seem to equate land, place, and home.

Keahey aligns the more mystically phrased notions of home as language, home as poetry, and home as contemplation, with more socially oriented ideas of home as culture. She draws on Edward Said's conceptualizing of "'home' in different 'places'" (4). As well, she cites John Berger's notions of home as "a set of practices" that acquire value through sheer repetition. She quotes Berger to say that "home is no longer a dwelling but the untold story of a life being lived" (6). Such notions of "repeated practices" and "culture" and "untold stories" being, in a broader sense, what determines a concept of "home" are made more necessary by realties of migration (immigration) and the ethnic map, and what is foregrounded is the poet's "social, psychological, and cultural relationship" (7) to space and to place. In light of these broad, socially determined features of the idea of home, the conceptualizations voiced by McKay and Lilburn are further steps in the same direction, but made mystical and, in a curious way, hermitic. The poet goes through the culturally determined relationships and out into the solitude, which takes him back to the land in a more mystical way.

The idea that the poet is able to take the whole panorama of "cultural practices" and linguistic usage into the contemplative and hermitic, Keahey notes, is closer to a comment made by Milton Wilson, whom she refers to in her study. Keahey quotes Wilson to the effect that the idea of home is, more than a place, a "direction, an attraction—something like the movement of a compass needle; not where it is, but where it points matters" (10). The poet taps this magnetism or energy, as we see in Szymborska, Tsvetaeva, and Broumas, and what is tapped is the poem itself. One writer who illustrates that combination of the social and the solitary fusing in "literary homemaking" is French novelist and essayist Marguerite Duras. Duras is not a poet as such, but her prose is so poetic that to talk of genre is just to quibble. Duras's last book is a collection of five essays, and the title essay, "Writing," is all about the relationship between poetry (writing) and home, in all the senses it has been talked about here. She writes about being at home in her house in Neauphle, but more than that, how she has found a home in the actual practice of writing. She explains that her "home" is not where she sleeps or eats and so forth, but it is anywhere where she can write: "It's a certain window, a certain table, habits of black ink, untraceable marks of black ink, a certain chair. And certain habits that I always maintain, wherever I go, wherever I am, even in places where I don't write, such as hotel rooms" (3). Here we have the "compass point" and the "direction" which constitute home for the poetic impulse.

As illustrated in Szymborska's poem "Going Home," home is for the poetic impulse an attitude, a posture, a personal habit, which has everything to do with the act of writing. Home is also a primeval memory, brought on by confrontations with images and sensations in nature. Wherever you look in the world, it seems, this perspective that binds a notion of home and belonging with a memory, an attitude, an atmosphere, and all of this with something in nature, is drawn up by poets again and again. For example, the much-loved Swedish poet Edith

Södergran (1892-1923), a lyricist of intense feeling, writes in her poem
"Homecoming," which appeared in her 1925 collection *The Land That
Is Not There*, of returning home after being away for a long time:[9]

> My childhood tree stands jubilantly around me: Human being!
> And the grass greets me welcome from foreign lands.
> I bend my head to the grass: finally home.
> Now I turn my back to everything that lies behind me:
> My new friends will be the wood and the beach and the sea.
> Now I will drink wisdom from the crowns of sap-filled branches,
> Now I drink strength from the smallest and youngest blade of grass:
> A great protector reaches out to me a merciful hand. (183, my
> translation)

It is not certain whether the narrator has returned physically to the
landscape of her childhood, but that question becomes secondary.
What the poem says, much like Marina Tsvetaeva's, is that when culture, society, city life, or even language fail to sustain the inner spirit,
which is the poetic spirit, she turns to "the wood and the beach and
the sea" for strength and comfort. Beyond that childhood landscape,
which the poem cannot actually articulate, the poet's particular seed
of sustenance becomes the poem itself, the utterance of that source
of comfort.

I will attempt to end all of this talk of home and wilderness and
poetry with a poem of my own on the same subject. The title poem
from *Silence of the Country* is narrated by someone who is at home but
does not really believe it. She has a sense of unreality about her hold
on the place she lives in, her ability to possess and keep it, and thinks
it may be lost, stolen, or swept away from her. Nothing is secure, and
at the same time, in order for this poem to exist at all, the narrator has
to recognize that insecurity is fundamental to poetic hearing, and needs
to be embraced. Her problem is not really with home, but with being
able to write: because between her and writing there is a glass wall,
just as in the poem there is a window pane between her standing inside
and the wilderness outside, which she is looking at:

> I tell myself this is home
> remind myself, as if otherwise
> forgotten, a memory blackout, so I say
>
> my oakwood table, my white office lamp
> from the village store, my pictures
> the ones I ask no one else to like

my stained glass windows on chains
even the green beeswax candles, mine
in brass candelabras with long legs

as if it could be taken away, perhaps by love
or some twist of fate
it has often been said nothing is secure

not even the view, the still
vision of Mount Khartoum, snow-
dusted green hills going down

into mauve water, not even this
vision from my window is sure
and I knock on the glass to hear a sound.

# Notes

1 Jacques Dupin is a noted French poet and art critic, born in 1927; editor of the journal *L'Ephémère*, and director of publication for the Galerie Maeght in Paris. Dupin, whose work is described as being both quiet and risky, has exerted an influence on poetry in the United States.

2 Hugo Ball (1886-1927) was born in Switzerland and was co-founder of the Zurich Dada movement. He was an anti-war agitator and sound poet and became co-editor of the newspaper *Freye Zeitung* in Bern. Auster is quoting from Hugo Ball's *Flight Out of Time: A Dada Diary*, ed. John Elderfield, trans. Ann Raimes.

3 Giuseppe Ungaretti (1888-1970) was an influential Italian poet and lecturer in literature. He was born in Alexandria, Egypt, but his family was from Lucca in Tuscany, Italy. He studied at the Sorbonne in Paris, where he lived until 1914, when he returned to Italy and was forced to join the army, after which he returned to Paris. He went back to Italy in 1942 and became a professor of modern Italian literature at the University in Rome. He died in Milan.

4 The argument is increasingly put forward in the public and in the media that finding "still points" in our hurried life is generally good for your health. As an example of that, the popular alternative health guru Deepak Chopra counsels the wisdom of meditation as the best preventive measure against illness, next to exercise. A recent book by Davis Kundtz, titled *How to Be Still When You Have to Keep Going* (Berkeley, CA: Conari Press, 1990) tackles the problem of how to go about this. The book is written by a former cleric who developed the idea of three degrees of "stillness" in a busy life. One is "still points," another "stopover," and a third is "grinding halt." A "still point" is just stopping for a moment and doing nothing. A "stopover" is longer, like taking a walk in the woods. A "grinding halt" is a total vacation— the kind of retreat offered by St. Peter's Benedictine Abbey in Saskatchewan, and this can last for as long as a few months at a time.

5 Jostein Gaarder is a Norwegian writer, born in 1952 in Oslo. He is a former philosophy teacher who became internationally known for his novel *Sophie's World*. Gaarder's experience is similar to Coelho and even Rowling: they have written books that break all the rules and are wildly popular at the same time, defying the odds.

6   Christa Wolf (b. 1929) is a German literary critic, novelist, and essayist, and is both controversial and experimental. Her work mixes fiction, essay, and auto-biography, and her narratives are considered demanding and complex. Some of the issues she writes about are nuclear holocaust, Germany's Nazi past, feminism, and exile. She came under criticism for collaborating with the former GDR—public criticism which she is said to be slowly overcoming.

7   Laura Riding (1901-1991) was born in Reichenthal in New York and began publishing poetry in 1923. She went to England at the age of twenty-four and wrote twenty books in the next thirteen years abroad, as well as a collaboration with Robert Graves, *A Survey of Modernist Poetry* and *A Pamphlet Against Anthologies*. She married Schuyler B. Jackson in 1941, with whom she collaborated on the publication *Rational Meaning: A New Foundation for the Definition of Words*. She was a member of the Fugitive Group and she was awarded the Bollingen Prize for poetry in 1991.

8   See his essay "After Soweto" in the same book.

9   He refers to Samuel Beckett here as an example of an author who has "reduced visual and linguistic elements to a minimum" (95).

10  Edmond Jabès (1912-1991), of an Italian Jewish family, was born in Cairo, married Arlette Cohen in 1935, and was forced to leave Cairo in 1956 because of Nasser's nationalist crackdown. He is widely regarded as one of the foremost poets of the twentieth century. In 1957 he moved to Paris where he remained until he died. *The Book of Questions* is a work in seven volumes, produced between 1963 and 1973, and is considered his main work, and was, according to the author, part of a larger production which included his three-volume work *The Book of Resemblances*.

11  Marguerite Duras (1914-1996), was French, but was born in Gia Dinh, Indochina (Vietnam) where she spent most of her childhood. She worked for a while as a secretary at the ministry of colonies, and was a member of the French Resistance during World War II. She joined the Communist Party, whose policies she later condemned. She is internationally known for her fiction, plays, and screenplays, in particular *Hiroshima Mon Amour* and *India Song*. She married Robert Antelme, a Holocaust survivor. She was associated with the New Novel group.

## Chapter Two

1   Mario Vargas Llosa was born in Arequipa in 1936. He grew up in Cochabamba, Bolivia, in Piura, northern Peru, and in Lima. He married Julia Urquidi in 1955, a marriage that ended in 1964. He went to graduate school at the University of Madrid in Spain, and wrote on Garcia Marquez and later Flaubert. He has received many prizes for his fiction and criticism. His novels include *The Time of the Hero, Aunt Julia and the Scriptwriter, The Green House, The War at the End of the World, The Real life of Alejandro Mayta,* and *The Storyteller.*

2   I do not distinguish here between "levels" or "intensities" of the diasporic experience, but instead survey what writers have said diaspora means to

their writing. Differentiations involving race, religion, exile, the experience of the refugee from war or persecution are matters that need to be discussed in other essays and cannot be covered here. I am treating "diaspora" as a base-line condition, and am not attempting to "erase" important distinctions within the diasporic milieu. My emphasis is exclusively on the writer.

3   Quoted in Ray Conlogue, "The double life of Nancy Huston," in the *Globe and Mail*, Wednesday, 3 November 1999, C2.

4   Paul Celan (1920-1970) was born in Czernowitz, Romania (now Ukraine), named Paul Antschel. He lost his parents to Nazi deportation and was himself in a German forced labour camp and suffered under Soviet occupation. He lived in Paris after the war, but had mental problems as a result of his experiences and took his own life by drowning himself in the Seine River in the spring of 1970.

5   André Brink was born in South Africa in 1935. His novels include *A Dry White Season, A Chain of Voices, An Act of Terror, The First Life of Adamastor, On the Contrary,* and *Imaginings of Sand.* He has won the CAN Award three times and been shortlisted for the Booker Prize twice.

6   John Gardner was born in 1933 in Batavia, New York, and died in 1982 in a motorcycle accident, only forty-nine years old. His novels include *Grendel* and *October Light.* He taught creative writing, and was a poet, dramatist, and translator as well as a novelist and teacher.

7   Francisco de Quevedo y Villegas (1580-1645), born in Madrid, studied with the Jesuit order and at the University of Alcala. He lived in Madrid, and later in Italy, and then back in Spain. Some of his books were censured by the Inquisition in the early 1600s. He is known for his poems and essays, and was imprisoned for political reasons in 1639.

8   Leslie Poles Hartley (1895-1972) was a novelist, short story writer, and critic. He is best known for his trilogy of novels *The Shrimp and the Anemone, The Sixth Heaven,* and *Eustace and Hilda.* His novel *The Go-Between* was made into a successful film.

9   A "homeland" in the South African context is the creation of small, quasi-sovereign nation states, by the white government, between the 1960s and 1980s, under the 1951 Bantu Authorities Act. As such, the white government set aside 13 percent of South African territory and turned it into regions of black home rule. These regions were called homelands, meaning the other 87 percent of South Africa was white territory.

10   Saul has a lengthy argument on the subject of language here. His main point is that we have separated public language from private, corporate language. Corporate language makes itself obscure and impenetrable in order to close its walls to outsiders and thus control the masses with it. "Obscurity suggests complexity which suggests importance," he writes, and what he calls corporatist dialects make language a weapon of power (49).

11   It is Eudora Welty who points out the absurdity of the problem of "accuracy" in fiction by mentioning in her essay "Place in Fiction" that "There

will still be the lady, always, who dismissed *The Ancient Mariner* on the grounds of implausibility" (117).

## CHAPTER THREE

1   Pierre Bonnard (1867-1947), French painter, one of the first artists to use pure colour in flat patterns and decorative arabesques. He was a member of the group known as the Nabis, precursors of the art nouveau style.

2   Bessie Head (1937-1986) was one of Africa's most prominent writers. Her mother was Scottish and her father was black, and she was raised in a foster home in South Africa until she was thirteen. She attended missionary school and became a teacher, and then a journalist writing for the *Golden City Post*. In 1964 she worked as a teacher in Botswana, where she remained in "refugee" status for fifteen years, eventually gaining citizenship. Her three major novels are *When Rain Clouds Gather, Maru,* and *A Question of Power.*

3   Quoted in James Fenton, "A Room of One's Own," review of *The Scholar in His Study: Ownership and Experience in Renaissance Italy,* by Dora Thornton (*New York Review of Books,* 13 August 1998, 53).

4   Leslie Marmon Silko was born in 1948 and raised in the Laguna Pueblo, west of Albuquerque, New Mexico. She is of mixed heritage—white, Mexican, and Native American. She graduated from the University of Albuquerque and worked as professor at the University of Tucson, Arizona. Her books include *Gardens in the Dunes, Almanac of the Dead, Yellow Woman and a Beauty of the Spirit: Essays on Native American Life Today, Ceremony,* and *Storyteller.*

5   Marsilio Ficino (1433-1499) was a Florentine, and it is said he never set foot outside of Florence in his lifetime. Ficino was a priest, a doctor, and a musician, but best known for his translations of classic works. He led the Florentine Platonic Academy and was important to the rediscovery of classical learning in the Renaissance.

## CHAPTER FOUR

1   Lee Maracle is of Salish and Cree ancestry and a member of the Sto:loh Nation, born 1950 in North Vancouver, BC. Her books include *Sojourner's Truth, Sundogs, Ravensong, Bobbi Lee, Daughters Are Forever, Will's Garden, Bent Box,* and *I Am Woman.*

2   Bharati Mukherjee, born in Calcutta, India, in 1940, moved to Britain in 1947 with her family. She acquired a BA from the University of Calcutta, and an MA from the University of Baroda in 1961. She went to the University of Iowa on a scholarship and earned an MFA in creative writing in 1963 and a PhD in English in 1969. She married Clark Blaise, well-known Canadian writer, in 1963. She became professor at the University of California at Berkeley. Her works include *The Tiger's Daughter, Wife, An Invisible Woman, Darkness, Jasmine, The Holder of the World,* and *Leave It to Me.*

3 Victor Segalen (1878-1919), French marine officer, poet, and travel writer. He is known for his critique of ethnocentrism, colonialism, and exoticism. He is best known for his novel *Les Immémoriaux*, a book about Tahiti, and his travel narratives of China, including *Equipée*.

4 Arthur Golden, according to publicity associated with this book, actually earned degrees in Japanese art and history from Harvard and Columbia, and an MA in English, and he is said to have spent ten years researching geisha culture, relying heavily on the information of Mineko Iwasaki, a geisha herself.

5 Robert Bringhurst was born in Los Angeles in 1946 and resides in Canada. He received a BA from Indiana University in 1973 and an MFA from UBC in 1975. He has written extensively on West Coast artist Bill Reid. His books include *Deuteronomy, The Beauty of the Weapons, Pieces of Map, Pieces of Music*, and *The Calling*. See *A Story as Sharp as a Knife: The Classical Haida Mythtellers and Their World* (Vancouver: Douglas & McIntyre, 2000).

6 Susan Richards Shreve has written twelve novels and several children's books. She is a long-time teacher of writing and is the founder of the MFA program in creative writing at George Mason University.

7 The prospect of an author "colonizing" herself or "appropriating" from herself or her own culture and investing the life of another culture with those borrowings is something well worth looking at separately. I have begun such a reading of transcultural translations in my essay "Life as Fiction: Narrative Appropriation in Isak Dinesen's *Out of Africa*." In *Isak Dinesen and Narrativity: Reassessments for the 1990s*, ed. Gurli A. Woods (Ottawa: Carleton University Press, 1994).

8 Ha Jin was born in Liaoing, China, in 1956. He spent his childhood in China during the Cultural Revolution, and at fourteen joined the army and spent six years as a soldier. His books include *Ocean of Words, Under the Red Flag, In the Pond*, and *Waiting*, as well as the volumes of poetry *Between Silences* and *Facing Shadows*. He now lives in the United States and teaches at Emory University in Atlanta.

9 Kazuo Ishiguro was born in Nagasaki, Japan, in 1954 and moved to Britain in 1960. He attended the University of Kent at Canterbury and the University of East Anglia. His novels include *A Pale View of Hills, An Artist of the Floating World, The Remains of the Day*, and *When We Were Orphans*.

10 Chang-rae Lee was born in Seoul, Korea, in 1965. He moved to the United States with his family at the age of three, and was raised in Westchester, New York. He graduated from Yale in English, and from the University of Oregon with an MFA in writing. His novels include *Native Speaker* and *A Gesture Life*. He lives in New York and is director of the MFA program at Hunter College.

11 Dennis Lee was born in Toronto in 1939, and was raised in Toronto. His books include *Civil Elegies, Kingdom of Absence, Riffs*, and *Nightwatch: New and Selected Poems 1968-1996*. Interestingly, neither Ha Jin, Maxine Hong Kingston, Chang-rae Lee, nor Kazuo Ishiguro exhibit the uses of

"interlanguage" (Ashcroft 66-68) that accompanies postcolonial texts. Nonetheless, Amy Tan has written about her own discovery of "interlanguage" when she finds she may write English with an accent, and may use the Chinese-English of her mother as a dialect without having it read as "broken English" or as mistaken English.

### Chapter Five

1 I find these comments of hers to be ill informed, but representative of a populist view that is common. Popular literature and literature worth investigating for complexity of idea and structure are not the same, nor are they meant to be. The analogy with music is good: should classical music that is complex and challenging be disavowed simply because it is not popular? The contention in this chapter will be that challenging writing is far from "elitist," as it is sometimes described, but is instead the fruit of serious work and its lack of popularity in general says nothing about its value. "Challenging" writing could include hypertexts and postmodern texts, as well as other genres not easily understood.

2 Saul's argument in this collection of five Massey lectures is understandable, because he links the uses of specialized rhetoric to politics, and claims that obscure language is used in the service of fascist corporatism, and against true democracy. However, he might be said to throw away the baby with the bathwater because there are certain experiences in human thought that do require a language that will fit them. The difference is between true investigations into language and communication, as opposed to using language for purposes of exclusion, power, and propaganda. It is our job to sort such uses out; not all specialized language is exclusionary. An argument should never be made against the refined and nuanced use of language to articulate human thought.

3 Kroetsch goes on to say that "It is because they don't exist that one can be original," but hastens to add that is not really an argument, in so many words, for the possibility of originality. It is, instead, a matter of redefining the idea of originality, which he does not get into further.

4 The first of three Wellec Library Lectures in Critical Theory, given at the University of California, Irvine, under the auspices of the Critical Theory Institute, in May 1990. Published as *Three Steps on the Ladder of Writing*.

5 An interesting essay on the subject of lying in fiction is Mario Vargas Llosa's essay "The Truth of Lies," included in his book *Making Waves: Essays by Mario Vargas Llosa*.

### Chapter Six

1 Antonin Artaud was born in Marseilles in 1896 and died in Paris in 1948. He started as a surrealist but had a falling out with Breton and went his own way after that. He is best known for his poems and essays, and he also acted on the stage and in movies. He was in a mental asylum from 1937 to 1946

and is reported to have undergone fifty-one electroshock treatments. Artaud has been very influential to other writers and artists, and continues to be so.

2  George Oppen (1908-1984) was born in New York into the Oppenheimer family. He was expelled from the military academy in 1925 and was suspended from Oregon State University as well. He married Mary Colby in 1927 and moved to New York. He was a part of the "objectivist" movement in American poetry (a label he denied). He moved to France in 1929 and returned three years later. Together with Zukofsky, Reznikoff, and Williams, Oppen helped create the Objectivist Press. He joined the Communist Party and moved to Mexico in 1950, renouncing poetry for eight years. In 1969 he received the Pulitzer Prize for *Of Being Numerous*. He spent a year in Israel in 1975. His *Collected Poems* was published in 1975, and his last collection, *Primitive*, in 1978.

3  Ben Okri was born in Lagos, Nigeria, in 1959. He published his first book *Flowers and Shadows* in 1979, and then *Landscapes Within* in 1981, *Incidents of the Shrine* in 1985, *Stars of the New Curfew* in 1987, *The Famished Road*, which won him the Booker Prize, and *Songs of Enchantment*. Other books include *Astonishing the Gods, Dangerous Love*, and a book of poems, *Birds of Heaven*. He has won the Commonwealth Writers Prize and the Aga Khan Prize for Fiction, among other awards.

## CHAPTER SEVEN

1  Barry Hannah was born in Mississippi in 1942 and did graduate work in Arkansas. His books include *Airships, Captain Maximus, Hey Jack!, Boomerang, Never Die, Bats Out of Hell*, and *High Lonesome*.

2  Anne Michaels was born in Toronto in 1958. Her books include *Fugitive Pieces, Miner's Pond*, and *The Weight of Oranges*. She has been awarded the Commonwealth Prize, the Canadian Authors' Association Award, the Orange Prize, and the Trillium Book Award for her work.

3  While you could argue that a novel like *War and Peace* is both very long and intense, the intensity does not bear down on every word or utterance there, as it does in Elizabeth Smart's case.

4  My own books, *The Prowler, The Substance of Forgetting, Zero Hour, The Rose Garden*, and *Night Train to Nykobing*, are all derived from the style of writing I am discussing here. The last-mentioned of these titles is a writerly response to Lispector's *The Stream of Life* in a very direct way.

5  James M. Cain's novel *The Postman Always Rings Twice*, about a wayfarer who ends up working at a gas station for a Greek and his young wife, and who ends up collaborating with the wife to kill her husband, and undergoes a trial and sentencing for a crime that appears truly senseless, is another short novel that fits in with this discussion. Cain's novel is apparently, according to Camus himself, a direct inspiration for *The Outsider*. It is James Cain who created the American *film noir* genre of scriptwriting, and the connection between the short, intense novel and the noir cinema needs to be explored.

6   Abdelkebir Khatibi is the author of many books, including (English titles) *To Think the Maghreb, A Summer in Stockholm, The Same Book, The Book of Blood.* He was born in Morocco in 1938. He has been a professor at the Mohammed V University in Rabat.

7   Susanna Tamaro was born in Trieste, and is the author of six books of fiction and non-fiction, including a memoir titled *Turning Home* and four children's books. She lives in Umbria.

8   Alessandro Baricco was born in Turin in 1958. He started out as a music critic and journalist. His novels include *Oceano Mare, Seta,* and *City.* He is the founder of a writing school called The Holden.

9   Paulo Coelho was born in Rio de Janeiro in 1947. He is considered a mass cultural phenomenon, his books receiving near-cult status all over the world. His works have been translated into fifty-six languages and have been on bestseller lists in numerous countries. His books include *Veronika Decides to Die, The Fifth Mountain, The Pilgrimage,* and *By the River Piedra I Sat Down and Wept.*

## CHAPTER EIGHT

1   Wislawa Szymborska was born in 1923 in Kornik, Poland, and has lived in Krakow since 1931. She studied Polish literature and sociology at the Jagiellonian University and was poetry editor of *Zycie Literackie* from 1953 to 1981. She has published sixteen collections of poetry and was awarded the Goethe Prize in 1991, the Herder Prize in 1995, and the Nobel Prize in 1996, as well as the Polish PEN Club prize. "Going Home" appeared in her 1962 collection *Salt* (reprinted in English in *Poems New and Collected, 1957-1997*).

2   Marcel Beyer was born in 1965, grew up in Cologne, and later moved to Dresden. His books include *Nonfiction, The Karnau Tapes,* and *Spione.* He has been called an avant-garde "ventriloquist" and has won several literary prizes.

3   See my essay, "Translation as Appropriation" in *Canada and the Nordic Countries,* ed. G. Gudsteins (Reykjavik: University of Iceland, 2001).

4   Marina Ivanova Tsvetaeva (1892-1941) is considered one of the most original Russian poets of the twentieth century, whose work saw a revival during the 1960s. Her father, Ivan Tsvetayev, was a professor of art history and the founder of the Museum of Fine Arts, and her mother Mariya (née Meyn) was a concert pianist. Marina was educated in Switzerland, Germany, and France, and began publishing poetry at the age of eighteen. She married Sergei Efron in 1912 and had two daughters and one son. During the Moscow famine in 1917, one of her daughters died of starvation. Tsvetaeva produced a large body of work.

5   *Vertical Man Horizontal World* is a term used by Canadian scholar Laurie Ricou and the title of his book-length study of Canadian prairie writing.

6   Olga Broumas was born in Syros, Greece, and moved to the United States as a young woman. She earned a BA in architecture from the University of Pennsylvania and an MFA in creative writing from the University of Oregon.

She received a Guggenheim fellowship and a National Endowment for the Arts grant. She has taught poetry writing at many colleges and universities and plays the jazz saxophone. Her poetry publications include *Caritas, Beginning with O, Sappho's Gymnasium, Eros, Eros, Eros,* and *Rave.*

7   John Berryman, one of the United States' best-known poets, was born in Oklahoma in 1914, and attended Columbia College and Cambridge University. He was a professor at the University of Minnesota. His publications include *The Dispossessed, Homage to Mistress Bradstreet,* and *The Dream Songs.* He was awarded the Pulitzer Prize for *77 Dream Songs.* He jumped off a bridge in Minneapolis in 1972 and drowned.

8   Zbigniew Herbert (1924-1998) was born in Poland. He graduated from the University of Krakow with an MA in economics in 1947, and from the Nicholas Copernicus University of Torun with an MA in law the following year. He earned a third MA from the University of Warsaw in 1950, in philosophy. He was a member of the Polish Resistance during World War II. He won many literary prizes during his lifetime, including the Nicholaus Lenau Prize and the Jerusalem Literature Prize. His books include *Selected Poems* (1968 and 1977), *The Barbarians in the Garden, Report from a Besieged City, Still Life with a Bridle, Mr. Cogito, The King of the Ants,* and *Elegy for the Departure.*

9   Edith Södergran is regarded as one of Finland's greatest modern poets. She wrote in Swedish, and her poems are lyrical and imagistic, visionary and intense, often compared to Rimbaud. She was born in 1892 into a Finno-Swedish family and grew up in Raivola and educated in St. Petersburg. She first wrote in German and was influenced by German romantic poetry, and later by Russian poets like Blok, Mayakovsky, and Severyanin. She contracted TB in 1908 and spent much of her adult life in sanatoria in Finland and Switzerland. Her work is collected under the title *Complete Poems.*

# Works Cited

Achebe, Chinua. *Hopes and Impediments, Selected Essays.* New York: Doubleday, 1989.

Adorno, Theodor W. *Critical Models, Interventions and Catchwords.* Translated by Henry W. Pickford. New York: Columbia University Press, 1998.

Almond, Jan. "Lessons from Kipling and Rao: How to Re-appropriate Another Culture." *Orbis Litterarum* 57 (2002): 275-87.

Arendt, Hannah, ed. *Walter Benjamin, Illuminations.* Translated by Harry Zorn. New York: Schocken, 1969.

Aschcroft, Bill, Gareth Griffiths, and Helen Tiffin. *The Empire Writes Back: Theory and Practice in Post-colonial Literatures.* London: Routledge, 1989.

Auster, Paul. *The Art of Hunger.* New York: Penguin, 1997.

Bainbridge, Beryl. *A Quiet Life.* London: Duckworth, 1999.

Bakhtin, M.M. *The Dialogic Imagination, Four Essays.* Edited by Michael Holquist, translated by Michael Holquist and Caryl Emerson. Austin: University of Texas Press, 1981.

Barthes, Roland. *The Pleasure of the Text.* Translated by Richard Miller. New York: Farrar, Strauss, and Giroux, 1975.

_____. *Writing Degree Zero.* Translated by Annette Lavers and Colin Smith. New York: Hill and Wang, 1968.

Bell, Madison Smartt. *Narrative Design. A Writer's Guide to Structure.* New York: Norton, 1997.

Benjamin, Walter. *Illuminations.* Edited by Hannah Arendt, translated by Harry Zorn. New York: Schocken, 1968.

Blanchot, Maurice. *The Blanchot Reader.* Edited by Michael Holland. Oxford: Blackwell, 1995.

Borges, Jorge Luis. *Seven Nights.* Translated by Eliot Weinberger. New York: New Directions, 1984.

Brink, André. *Writing in a State of Siege: Essays on Politics and Literature.* New York: Summit Books, 1983.

Broumas, Olga. *Rave, Poems 1975-1999.* Port Townsend: Copper Canyon Press, 1999.

## Works Cited

Butala, Sharon. "Telling the Truth." In *Landmarks*, edited by R. Birks, T. Eng, and J. Walchli, 7-13. Scarborough: Prentice Hall Allyn and Bacon, 1998.

_____. *The Perfection of the Morning*. Toronto: Harper Collins, 1994.

Butler, Judith. *Subjects of Desire: Hegelian Reflections in Twentieth-Century France*. New York: Columbia University Press, 1999.

Byatt, A.S. *The Biographer's Tale*. London: Vintage, 2000.

Calvino, Italo. *Six Memos for the Next Millennium*. Translated by Patric Ceagh. Toronto: Vintage, 1995.

Camus, Albert. *The Outsider*. Translated by Joseph Laredo. Harmondsworth: Penguin, 2000.

Cixous, Hélène. *Coming to Writing and Other Essays*. Edited by Deborah Jenson, translated by Sarah Cornell. London: Harvard University Press, 1991.

_____. *Three Steps on the Ladder of Writing*. Translated by Sarah Cornell and Susan Sellers. New York: Columbia University Press, 1993.

Coelho, Paulo. *The Alchemist*. Translated by Alan R. Clarke. New York: Harper Perennial, 1998.

_____. "The Coming of Age of a Brazilian Phenomenon: An Interview with Paul Coelho." *World Literature Today*. April-June 2003, 57-59.

Cuthbert, Denise. "Beg, Borrow or Steal: The Politics of Cultural Appropriation." Review of *Borrowed Power: Essays on Cultural Appropriation* by Bruce Ziff and Pratima V. Rao. *Postcolonial Studies* 1, no. 2 (1998): 257-62.

Daggy, Robert E., ed. *Thomas Merton, Day of a Stranger*. Salt Lake City: Gibbs M. Smith, 1981.

Deane, Seamus, ed. *James Joyce, Portrait of the Artist as a Young Man*. New York: Penguin, 1992

Derrida, Jacques. *Writing and Difference*. Translated by Alan Bass. Chicago: University of Chicago Press, 1978.

Dillard, Annie. *For the Time Being*. New York: Vintage, 1999.

_____. *The Writing Life*. New York: Harper Collins, 1989.

Duras, Marguerite. *Writing*. Translated by Mark Polizzotti. Cambridge: Lumen Editions, 1989.

Fenton, James. "A Room of One's Own." Review of *The Scholar in His Study: Ownership and Experience in Renaissance Italy* by Dora Thorton. *New York Review of Books* 13 August 1998, 52-53.

Gaarder, Jostein. *Sophie's World*. Translated by Paulette Moller. New York: Berkeley Books, 1996.

Gardner, John. *The Art of Fiction*. New York: Vintage, 1991.

Griffiths, Paul. "Don't Blame Modernists for Empty Seats." *New York Times* 22 March 1998, 37.

Hannah, Barry. "Speaking of Writing: 'Spies with Music'." In *The Tales We Tell, Perspectives on the Short Story* edited by Barbara Lounsberry, et al., 207-11. London: Greenwood, 1998.

Head, Bessie. *A Woman Alone: Autobiographical Essays.* Edited by Craig MacKenzie. London: Heinemann, 1990.

Herbert, Zbigniew. "Home." Translated by John and Bogdana Carpenter. *Kenyon Review* 21, no. 1 (Winter 1999): 19.

Hodgins, Jack. *A Passion for Narrative: A Guide for Writing Fiction.* Toronto: McClelland and Stewart, 1993.

hooks, bell. *Remembered Rapture.* New York: Henry Holt, 1999.

_____. *Teaching to Transgress: Education as the Practice of Freedom.* New York: Routledge, 1994.

Johnston, Ingrid. "Dilemmas of Identity and Ideology in Cross-Cultural Literary Engagements." *Canadian Ethnic Studies* 29 (1997): 97-108.

Jonas, George. "Café Society." *Saturday Night* 10 June 2000.

Joyce, James. *A Portrait of the Artist as a Young Man.* New York: Penguin, 1992.

Kauffman, Bill. "Passport to Main Street." *Utne Reader* July-August 2000, 53-55.

Keahey, Deborah. *Making It Home: Place in Canadian Prairie Literature.* Winnipeg: University of Manitoba Press, 1999.

Kennedy, Fraser. "A House on the North Sea." *Architectural Digest* May 1999, 44-45.

King, Stephen. *On Writing: A Memoir of the Craft.* New York: Pocket Books, 2000.

Khatibi, Abdelkebir. *Love in Two Languages.* Translated by Richard Howard. Minneapolis: University of Minnesota Press, 1990.

Kristeva, Julia. *Revolution in Poetic Language.* Translated by Margaret Waller. New York: Columbia University Press, 1984.

Kroetsch, Robert. *A Likely Story.* Red Deer: Red Deer College Press, 1995.

Lee, Dennis. "400: Coming Home." *boundary 2* 3, no. 1 (Fall 1974): 23.

Lilburn, Tim. "How to Be Here?" In *Poetry and Knowing: Speculative Essays and Interviews,* edited by Tim Lilburn, 161-76. Kingston: Quarry Press, 1995.

Lindbergh, Anne Morrow. *Gift from the Sea.* New York: Pantheon, 1983.

Llosa, Mario Vargas. "The Truth of Lies." Translated by John King. *Partisan Review* 3 (1997): 356-65.

_____. *A Writer's Reality.* Edited by Myron I. Lichtblau. New York: Houghton Mifflin, 1991.

Maracle, Lee. "Native Myths: Tricksters Alive and Crowing." In *Landmarks: A Process Reader,* edited by R. Birks, T. Eng, J. Walchli, 311-15. Scarborough: Prentice Hall Allyn and Bacon, 1998.

McKay, Don. "Baler Twine: Thoughts on Ravens, Home, and Nature Poetry." In *Poetry and Knowing: Speculative Essays and Interviews,* edited by Tim Lilburn, 17-28. Kingston: Quarry Press, 1995.

Merton, Thomas. *Day of a Stranger.* Salt Lake City: Gibbs M. Smith, 1981.

## Works Cited

Michaels, Anne. "Cleopatra's Love." In *Poetry and Knowing: Speculative Essays and Interviews*, edited by Tim Lilburn, 147-83. Kingston: Quarry Press, 1995.

Miller, Laura. "www.claptrap.com." *New York Times Book Review* 15 March 1998.

Moore, Thomas. *Care of the Soul*. New York: Harper Perennial, 1994.

Mukherjee, Bharati. "An Invisible Woman." In *Landmarks: A Process Reader*, edited by Roberta Birks, Tomi Eng, Julie Walchli, 324-31. Scarborough: Prentice Hall Allyn and Bacon, 1998.

Okri, Ben. *A Way of Being Free*. London: Phoenix House, 1997.

Ortolano, Glauco. "The Coming of Age of a Brazilian Phenomenon: An Interview with Paul Coelho." *World Literature Today* 77 (2003): 57-59.

Padovano, Anthony T. *The Human Journey; Thomas Merton: Symbol of a Century*. New York: Doubleday, 1984.

Ricou, Laurie. *Vertical Man / Horizontal World: Man and Landscape in Canadian Prairie Fiction*. Vancouver: University of British Columbia Press, 1973.

Rushdie, Salman. *Imaginary Homelands: Essays and Criticism 1981-1991*. London: Granta/Penguin, 1991.

Saul, John Ralston. *The Unconscious Civilization*. Toronto: Anansi, 1995.

Shreve, Susan Richards. "A Storyteller Finds Comfort in a Cloak of Anonymity." *New York Times* 27 August 2001, B1-2.

Silko, Leslie Marmon. "Breaking Down the Boundaries: 'Earth, Air, Water, Mind'." In *The Tales We Tell, Perspectives on the Short Story*, edited by Barbara Lounsberry, et al., 91-94. London: Greenwood Press, 1998.

Soloman, Deborah. "Pierre Bonnard at Le Canet: The Artist's World in the South of France." *Architectural Digest* March 1998, 46-53.

Stegner, Wallace. *On the Teaching of Creative Writing: Responses to a Series of Questions*. Edited by Edward Connery Lathem. Dartmouth: Montgomery Endowment, Dartmouth College, 1997.

Szymborska, Wislawa. *Poems New and Collected 1957-1997*. Translated by Stanislaw Baranczak and Clare Cavanagh. New York: Harcourt, 1998.

Tamaro, Susanna. *Follow Your Heart*. Translated by John Cullen. New York: Bantam Doubleday, 1994.

Tate, James. *The Route as Briefed*. Ann Arbor: University of Michigan Press, 1999.

Tsvetaeva, Marina. *Selected Poems*. Translated by Elaine Feinstein. Harmondsworth: Penguin, 1993.

Welty, Eudora. *The Eye of the Story: Selected Essays and Reviews*. New York: Vintage, 1983.

Wolf, Christa. *The Fourth Dimension*. Translated by Hilary Pilkington. New York: Verso, 1988.

Woolf, Virginia. "Professions for Women." In *Major Modern Essayists,* 2nd ed., edited by Gilbert H. Muller and Alan F. Crooks, 4-8. New Jersey: Prentice Hall, 1994.

Ziff, Bruce, and Pratima V. Rao, eds. *Borrowed Power: Essays on Cultural Appropriation.* New Brunswick, NJ: Rutgers University Press, 1997.